I act now under my own command

I hunt down and exterminate soulless monsters of unimaginable horror and vileness.

My foes have killed their own souls by violating the sacredness of life.

The devouring has begun again. Death is everywhere. I am going to stop it.

I am a weapon that works in concert with other weapons: human weapons.

I stand alone on the edge of creation to extend the limits of the possible.

I do what must be done.

MACK BOLAN
The Executioner

DON PENDLETON's EXECUTIONER

MACK BOLAN

The New War Book

A GOLD EAGLE BOOK FROM
W RLDWIDE

TORONTO • NEW YORK • LONDON • PARIS
AMSTERDAM • STOCKHOLM • HAMBURG
ATHENS • MILAN • TOKYO • SYDNEY

First edition March 1984

ISBN 0-373-61063-7

Special thanks and acknowledgment to
Wiley Slade, Aaron Hill and Judy A. Newton
for their contributions to this work.

Printed in Canada

"Unless one comes to an understanding
concerning the nature of Change, one will
have many difficulties."

—*Plato*

"The possibility of victory by the dark
forces stands as black as night, fierce as ten
thousand furies, terrible as hell. Yet I am
not afraid to admit my fear. Courage is
resistance to fear, mastery of fear—not
absence of fear."

—*Mack Bolan*

Dedicated to the memory of April Rose.

CONTENTS

The New War

by Don Pendleton

Mack Bolan is at his headquarters base in Virginia, not far from Washington, D.C. It is a large farm in Blue Ridge country—Stony Man Farm, he calls it. By helicopter or fast car it is only minutes from the Pentagon, CIA headquarters or the White House.

The farm house and outbuildings contain a wealth of sophisticated electronic and computer facilities, all on 160 acres. The base lacks nothing in equipment and information; it has everything needed to back up Mack Bolan as Colonel John Phoenix in his New War.

April Rose is there this day. So are the three members of Able Team: Rosario Blancanales, Hermann Schwarz, Carl Lyons.

But events wait for no man. A major problem has arisen that must be handled immediately, before all the wires are connected, before all the pieces are in place.

The mission is NOW.

The man is Bolan.

Alone.

Bolan will be transported by helicopter into a predetermined jungle drop zone.

He will have only forty-eight hours from drop to pickup. During that period of time he must find a man called Laconia...or be totally on his own for as long as two weeks, because the area is about to be socked in with a tropical storm.

SO BEGAN MY DIRECTIVE at the beginning of The Executioner's New War. The Mafia lay in ruins, and Bolan prepared for his latest arduous mile. Glorious courage and success lay ahead, but so did pain and searing tragedy. Bolan was ready for it all.

And what a mile it's been. Starting with *The New War*, the thirty-ninth title since the story of Mack's life first appeared in print, John Phoenix's Terrorist Wars have taken the night-scorcher to Colombia, Turkey, Algeria, Vietnam, Germany, England, Libya, Nicaragua, Italy, Japan, Monaco, Zaire and Thailand—not to mention St. Paul, Washington, D.C., the Everglades, San Francisco, Idaho's River of No Return, the Colorado Rockies, the coast of Maine and Southern California.

And what is it that he gets at the end of his restless travail? By God, he gets Pittsfield revisited.

My memory is haunted by this past period in Mack's life. I think you'll agree that the Terrorist Wars have been charged with a special mix of fire and caring—a *burning* that has branded itself into Bolan's soul. It is a burning that cannot be tempered, a brand that cannot be removed. Bolan feels personally the wounds of every innocent victim of terror. And he feels another pain in addition, a terrible gnawing at his inner being caused by the very need to do the things that he does. He does not wage war against terrorists as a hobby. He is inflamed with the need to fight the enemy and protect the world. And that hurts—it has to. It has to be hell. Who would actually put himself in Mack's place and expose himself to such a terribly savage and bloody crusade of years?

Damn, just thinking about the guy gives me that feeling of anticipation, the stomach rising in the rib cage, that I got from every war-room scene when each deadly mission was set up. Whoever knew, even at the typewriter, how the hell it was going to turn out?

I can see the scene in my mind's eye. . . .

JOHN PHOENIX, whose "reconstructed identity" buried the longest and bloodiest campaign against organized crime the world had ever seen, a war raged furiously and shatteringly by one Mack Bolan, ex-sergeant, U.S.A., known by the entire world as The Executioner, entered the War Room at the farm.

The lady in the war room could have been an actress or glamour model but was neither. Voted "the solid-state physicist most likely to go to Hollywood" by her graduating class, she was April Rose, a Justice Department technical operative when first encountered by Bolan, now Stony Man Chief of Operations and soulmate to the boss.

April worked her trick at the terminal. Brognola lit a cigar and sighed. He held the cigar in stained fingers as he leaned forward to peer at the fast-moving ground track of computer lines rippling endlessly across the screen, reproducing terrain features as though viewed through the window of an extremely fast aircraft.

The display had the eerie quality of time-lapse photography, though it was not that. It was a computer-enhanced photograph of the entire continent, shot from a "spy" satellite orbiting high above the earth, broken down and spit out in piecemeal sequences as selected by the computer program. Bolan, too, gazed at the screen, his eyes clouded with some phantasmal emotion.

"Is it max mag?" he asked.

"From this particular shot, yes," she replied. "Higher magnification will only blur what details we can see now."

April ordered a new shot on the screen. Brognola stood and stretched, then cast a friendly gaze at Bolan and said, "Able Team gets this one, eh?"

Bolan nodded. "Duck soup for those guys. They know what it is to tie close numbers."

April organized an immediate Able Team ordnance call-up on her keyboard. She smiled with relief at Bolan. "What else do you need, pal?"

He smiled back, matching her warmth. "If you have to ask, April . . . ."

He gently squeezed her arm, flicked an eye at Brognola and strode away before Brognola could stop him. The older man seemed about to say something, then checked himself.

"He's tired, Hal," April murmured, broodingly watching the retreating figure. "I'm glad Able Team can do this one for him."

"Course he's tired," the chief Fed grunted. "Superman would be tired with this job. But since when did I have any say over that guy?"

"He respects you, Hal."

"I know he does, and that's the hardest damn part of it." The high-ranking Fed glared at his cigar as if wondering where it came from.

"Just trust his instincts," April whispered.

"I trust him clear to the gates of hell," Brognola growled. Bolan was striding back into the war room, head down, his walk suggesting preoccupied thought. "That's why I . . . ." Brognola paused, waiting for Bolan to get closer, then brusquely announced, "That's why I think *you* should do this one, Striker. I know, I know, we just set it up differently, and you're tired, and I wouldn't ask . . . but no offense to Able, this is all just too damn—"

Bolan broke into that torture with a small smile and a flash of blue eyes just beginning to take on ice. "I think so, too," he said quietly. "Get me an override, Hal. Full contingencies, all of it. Seventh Fleet liaison. Air Force, all WestPac facilities, diplomatic support. Alert them all. I'm ready."

April turned to face him. "You don't owe anyone on this, Mack," she said.

"Owing has nothing to do with it," Bolan said. "I know how you feel, April, but I have to go. That's all there is to it. I have to."

April understood very well. It was one of the reasons she loved the man so. She resigned herself once again to a wild, wild battle of the heart, almost as devastating as bullets and bombs. Brognola softly left the room.

"I'll stand down Able Team," she murmured. "But I'll keep them on backup just in case. You need to talk to Hal. Go see him, Mack. Just kiss me, that's all."

He did, and then he went to talk to Hal.

With all hell waiting, worldwide.

Now April Rose is gone. It's 1984, and the world is falling to hell exactly the way Bolan has been saying it would.

What is it in Mack Bolan that makes him so prescient, so much the brother soldier whose singular path is a personal belief statement for the many? How in hell does he keep to his path, now that the flames are licking so unmercifully at his soul?

He is a very complex man, that's a start. He is faced with seemingly impossible challenges, always rising to them, never backing down except as a different route to the front; turning disadvantage to advantage, moving and closing in like a heat-seeking missile, yet all the while knowing that a victory merely condemns him to more hellfire.

I guess maybe only ten percent of what chugs through my mind when I'm writing finds its way onto the page. The stuff that stays in my head is the true inside story of Mack Bolan, the unseen dimension, which is perhaps only subliminally experienced by the reader.

For each of the Executioner books I have written, I could as easily have produced a book-length essay expanding the "inside" story of Bolan, the validation, the invisible stuff that provides the pressure of the story. In fact, more easily.

But instead, for practical purposes, I produced fictional adventures to allegorically present the same case.

The fact is that Mack's response to the highest call of duty has cost him everything that ever held peace in his heart. I have pointed out elsewhere that Mack is no kill-crazy goon, no arrogant superman glorying in his power over life and death. He is an often wearied and frightened and lonely and continually harassed human being who is simply doing a job that needs doing.

That job today is all the greater, global in scale, increasingly more dangerous and complex on a personal level. But never, neither in the Mafia wars nor the Terrorist Wars nor in the loneliest war of all that he fights now, has Mack Bolan been a zealot. Instead he is a man of titanic self-doubts, frequently overwhelmed by revulsion for the life of terror and gore that is his lot.

After sixty-two books, a character takes on an identity that I could not change if I wanted to. Bolan is Bolan as much as I am I. The world he inhabits has taken on its own identity, and it is the kind of world in which April Rose can be killed.

I have known Bolan in bits and pieces in many men. To find Mack Bolan in the real world would require only to fit the bits and pieces into a single personality, expose him to the same illuminations and challenges to which Bolan has been exposed, then sit back and watch the guy operate. Bolan is just a man. Certainly he could make it in the real world. I wish he were here. I wish he could avenge April's death for real.

In the sense that my principles and ethics may be striving toward some idealized goal of character—and in the sense that a fictional character is little different than an unrealized character in real life—yes, I suppose that Bolan and I are one.

But these books are not a fictionalized autobiographical series; I have not done the things Bolan has done. I do not have his expertise as a warrior. But if I did have his talents and if I then found myself in the same situation in which I have placed him in his fictional world, I would probably react as he has reacted.

In the spirit of realism, I have always made sure that Mack's battle engagements are possible—no, *probable*, considering the nature of the guy. At my homestead back in Nashville, Indiana, before I moved to California, I actually staged all my combat scenes and carefully ran through them, even if the scale of them took up all my forty acres. With the help of five old steel targets—two-dimensional men I salvaged from firing ranges— which ran on cables from place to place, I would be Bolan and I'd check how long it took me to get through the course, the number of rounds I could get off and the angle of fire. Sometimes I'd go through it from three different angles.

Such research is essential for our type of books and is now a central part of the Dolan saga. As a writer, I must always have a point of reference. More often than not, for example, Bolan shoots for the head. I know the chest is a better target, but if anybody can make a head hit it's Bolan; the death is quick, and a head shot doesn't leave hoodlums lying around dying from belly wounds, which would never be Mack's style.

IN THE NEW WAR, Bolan risked total war to exterminate the many-headed Hydra of world terrorism. He had to move his own kind of dirty war to the point where it went much further, beyond all sanction. And thus he risked rejection by every nation on earth, forcing himself to become a winged panther soaring over a cold ocean thousands of miles from home, moving through the crisp air for all time, unable to land.

But Bolan could not avoid the big fight. Remember how it went in *Stony Man Doctrine*? He and the other Stony Men raced from one country to another, from one battle to another, fighting terrorists, fighting mind-numbing fatigue, when they knew very well who sponsored, armed and paid the terrorists.

Yet they were unable to attack the nexus of terror. An attack by his men on the Kremlin meant overt and unconscionable war.

Instead, they had to hack off the thousands of devouring heads of the KGB's monstrous Department of Terror.

How costly has been this triumph?

When Bolan killed enemies in Vietnam, he was decorated for heroism. Then when he killed the enemy at home, he was charged with murder and hounded as a dangerous threat. Now he is about to be hounded once again, denounced as an international "criminal," a man without a country, doomed to live in a no-man's-land, never to know peace. It has been a hellish victory, and it has exacted the highest price.

But Bolan—his shivery presence still a wispy shadow in combat black, the only sound he makes the chilling wind that justifies all paranoia within the organized underworlds—will prevail.

I can state without fear of contradiction that Mack Samuel Bolan is a just man, an honorable man, a brave man. Despite his hour of grief, which we share so deeply with him, he will continue to react personally to the goons. Mack Bolan will prowl the savage streets, and he will civilize them—or will die trying.

That's the picture, sharp and clear. Now let's take time out and review how the latest books will be coming out in the stores. Major events are occurring in Bolan's life. Unprotected by government sanction, framed by his enemies, Mack Bolan is truly himself again, though through terrible loss.

These developments will appear in a trilogy, published more or less simultaneously with *The New War Book*, which has the MACK BOLAN name in red foil lettering on the cover of each of the three books, so that you can more readily identify them.

In Mack Bolan #62, *Day of Mourning*, Mack's greatest love and greatest ally, April Rose, is killed. She puts herself in the line of fire in a smash against Stony Man Farm.

This terrible event—far more grave than anything since Pittsfield, where Bolan's father shot himself and his wife and daughter when helplessly caught in the coils of mobsterism—propels The Executioner into *Terminal Velocity*, the new 384-page SuperBolan. It takes the blitzer to the rebel fastnesses of Afghanistan and thence to Moscow itself.

In the big book, Bolan becomes a hunted man, the target not only of his avowed enemies but the CIA as well. He acquires a new and deadly hazard to his life—Strakhov, the terror mobster, father of a test pilot Bolan has taken out in combat. To avenge his son, he will pursue Bolan to the ends of the earth, as surely as Bolan, to avenge those responsible for April's death, will pursue *him*.

Mack Bolan #64, *Dead Man Running*, the third book in the trilogy, tells how Bolan returns to launch an all-out attack against the vile hollowmen who smashed his base. His advance brings him to the Oval Office of the White House itself, where with his bare hands he takes an accounting for April Rose's death that leaves no room for debate. It is a big moment. By it, Mack consigns himself to a peculiar perdition—pardoned but outcast; a victorious fighter far more real to his president than ever before, yet beyond any further involvement with the U.S. government. It is an extraordinary time, bitter yet sad, hauntingly sad.

The glare of unrelenting terror remains, of course.

After all, Bolan is fighting for his name now.

And his name rings bells.

The *consiglieri* of a Family struggling to rebuild has witnessed Bolan's blitzkrieg in Washington. It is he who takes the news of Mack Bolan's return to the headshed in New York. . . .

In the middle of it all, we have Mack Bolan #63: *The New War Book*. This book is not just a new *War Book*, but a full and comprehensive look at the New War.

There are a couple of highly unusual stories in here I know you'll like. One of them, *Incident at Hoi Binh*, set back in Mack's Vietnam, shows the degree to which all wars are the same war when Sergeant Mercy comes across Nile Barrabas. Hell, this story even has a writer in it, a guy who has every intention of writing about Mack Bolan someday. . . . My thanks to Alan Bomack (the man responsible for *Terminal Velocity*) for the idea and Aaron Hill for the development of it. Aaron also worked on the Combat Catalog, along with Judy Newton, who drew the architectural and landscape elevations of Stony Man Farm and provided the Gallery of Characters; thanks Judy, for your very diligent work.

The Laser Wagon meets its fate in *Laser Raze*, a remarkable little piece (set toward the end of the terrorist wars) created by Wiley Slade, valued grunt on the line at Gold Eagle, who is a former intelligence officer assigned to the hottest Eastern Bloc country.

As for Mack's warpartners, the explosive Able Team and fearless Phoenix Force, make no mistake—Hal Brognola is going to hold the fort for those guys, and they're going to blast the world of terror apart. Carl, Pol and Gadgets admire Hal deeply and work well with him. Increasingly, Katz will take a role in the running of Stony Man Farm as it bounces back from its tragic hit.

The lineup in Gar Wilson's Phoenix Force is constantly imperiled by its very numbers, and future adventures will likely feature shocks on that front. Dick Stivers's Able Team fights on in fury, determined to hack its way into the heart of Central America's monstrous commu-nazism; but first for them, a secret mission to protect the Olympic Games in Los Angeles. Back to familiar war zones for Carl Lyons in particular!

You can expect Mack to operate alongside his men, on a *very* secret basis, at any time.

I SKETCHED AT THE OUTSET HERE the setup for the first Stony Man operation. In it I was creating the setting for a hero. Simply put, a hero is a person who rises beyond the ordinary levels of courage and resolution, beyond ordinary generosity and greatness of soul. The true hero invades the unconscious mind of his race. Indeed, in struggle and in symbol he enters the darkest and most perilous regions of human nature, where the real springs of character and action are born. It is there that the hero wins his victory and discovers truth.

What he discovers is *himself*, and he returns to the everyday world with a treasure that is hard to attain.

That treasure is integrity.

April, my love, you, too, are a hero

May you rest in peace.

Incident at Hoi Binh

Darkness hung like a shroud over the Vietnam jungle. Heavy rain clouds moved in from Laos, piling atop one another in a dark, swollen head. The afternoon was turned into a murky half-light, as if it were almost night.

Mack Bolan shifted gears as the jeep bounced along the muddy track. His hands and shirtfront were soaked with thick blood. His eyes were staring orbs. Near dawn he had stalked a Communist porter and killed him within earshot of a Vietcong squad. He had slit the enemy's throat and then held him close to muffle the sounds of his death, the man's death twitch a gruesome dance in the festival of hell they called the Vietnam War.

The operation was almost over. The battalion had been working for long days to clear villagers from the Steel Circle. The Army was about to turn the area into a free-fire zone, raining down artillery barrages at will to break the back of the VC operating in the region.

The big sergeant had discovered and reconned the supply routes that the coolies were using to bring arms and ammunition to the Vietcong. The Steel Circle was laced with a network of paths leading from the notorious Ho Chi Minh Trail into the piedmont, trails that snaked through the jungle, pulsing with bicycles, carts and sandaled feet.

The Steel Circle was a twenty-mile radius of jungle that Bolan's unit was fighting the VC for. It was not easy.

Led by a young guerrilla called the Green Dragon, the VC had been twisting through the swamp and village region making deadly hits with phantom accuracy. Bolan's company had been retaliating with all the Americans could swing in the way of speed, artillery and maneuverability. But the VC kept nagging them, somehow always staying one step ahead.

It was uncanny. The Green Dragon was like a ghost that could read the Americans' minds. And he always hit with merciless force, dealing every card of cruel destruction onto the green table of the region. It was not Bolan's first introduction to death and suffering, but it was the deepest. And he would never forget it.

He wanted the Green Dragon.

Bolan's main thrusts had been under cover of night. His waking hours were devoted to lonely missions into the heart of the Steel Circle, harassing porters, destroying VC squads and interrupting supply missions to the ruthless owners of the night. He moved silently through the jungle, hardly breathing, waiting and watching; he wanted the Green Dragon in his rifle sights.

But the guerrilla leader had managed to elude him. Bolan had spent nights hunting, sniping, harassing, but he had yet to find him. The daytime platoons had managed to evacuate all the villages in the Steel Circle but two. The next day the area would be a free-fire zone. Pounding artillery would blow the whole region into a battered, broken confusion.

Sergeant Bolan was tired. He tracked the VC in a state of self-induced hypnosis, his mind asleep in the sense that normal people know, and yet completely aware. His condition had only a distant relation to the normal world of the senses.

It had begun in the hellish eternity of nights in enemy territory, where the VC pursued him as purposefully as he pursued them. In the jungle, death whispered in the slightest rustling of leaves, lulling the sergeant's mind into modes no psychologist would touch.

He talked to death when it wrapped him in night. And he learned to empty his mind. nothing more. nothing less. He let the jungle talk to him, flow through him. A VC sniper, invisible to anyone else, was visible to Bolan. A mine planted in a paddy gave off an odor Bolan could smell.

It left him drained. As the operation wore on, Bolan would arrive back at camp looking more and more like the hollow-eyed reaper. He could see it in the way people stared at him. The cherries, the new recruits, would inevitably do a double take at the sight of him. Did the war do that to men?

If they lived that long, they would learn. Yeah, they would learn.

Bolan shifted gears again. He was approaching the camp, the temporary command post of his CO, Lieutenant Colonel Crawford. He was going to report on the night's mission, get a few hours of tortured sleep and then head back into the jungle.

One more lonely mission into the Steel Circle.

CRAWFORD'S HUT held an office strewn with maps and communications gear. It had been set up only two weeks before, yet it looked as if it had been used for months. Bolan found their Popular Forces guide, Nguyen, sitting with two civilians. Crawford was consulting with a red-faced major. He stopped talking when Bolan entered.

Without ceremony Bolan reported on the night's mission.

"Reconned the area around YD 34-58-36 and found two redball trails. One just had footprints, one or two days old. The other had considerable cart and bicycle tracks. Here and here," he said, tracing the routes on Crawford's map.

"How can you tell the difference between cart and bicycle tracks, Sergeant, when they both use bicycle wheels?" the major asked.

"Cart tracks come in pairs and are usually deeper," Bolan replied. He did not have time to waste educating the rear echelons. "I followed a Communist porter with a cartload of B-40 rounds and launchers. Tracked him to the rendezvous point then took him out." Bolan indicated the spot on the map. "But they won't be using it anymore. I sent the cart down the trail with four frags inside. No body count, sir. Too many secondaries. I estimate ten VC killed."

Crawford took it all in and nodded.

"Major," he said, turning to the portly officer, "this is my best penetration man." The major looked anew at Bolan. "You've done it again, Sergeant. Now get some rest. Tonight you're playing public-relations man for the war."

Bolan looked over to where the Vietnamese guide sat with the two civilians.

Crawford made the introductions. "Sergeant Bolan, this is Robert Hutton, a Canadian journalist. He's accompanying Nguyen this afternoon to observe Captain Nile Barrabas and his company clearing the villages of Hoi Binh and Ap Quan. Barrabas has already left. Nguyen is going to guide Hutton and catch up."

Bolan nodded to the correspondent, but felt an instant dislike. He had met the type so many times before. He was sure the civilian was a smartass on his first tour of Nam, his head full of clichés about what was going on.

"And this is Don Edelman. He's going to accompany you on your mission tonight." Bolan searched the man's face openly. It was a young face, clean and smooth, with eyes that met Bolan's.

"No way," Bolan said with quiet finality. "Sir."

"What's the matter, Sergeant?" said Hutton. "Don't you want the folks at home to see what you boys are doing over here?" Hutton thought he had caught Bolan, but Bolan didn't even look at him. He kept his eyes on Edelman.

"I'm not taking you for two reasons. First, I always move alone. Always. Five minutes in the jungle with you would announce our presence to the VC like a brass band. I don't want to carry your body all the way back here." He spoke with little emotion. "The second reason is this." Bolan reached over to Hutton. The journalist jumped back as if the big kill-smeared soldier was going to twist his head right off his shoulders. Bolan took him gently by the arm. "I want to show you something."

Bolan led the newsman outside to where he had parked the jeep. A soldier was just bending over the back, unfolding a body bag. Bolan told the private to take a break and then pulled the cover away. Edelman hung back a few feet. Hutton stood there uneasily. A foul smell of decay hovered over the back of the jeep.

"This is a Vietnamese girl, about eight years old. She was still breathing when I found her this morning. The rest of her family was dead; killed by the VC. I'm not going to tell you what they did to her but she didn't stay alive long. In fact, she died at my feet."

He gently brought Hutton closer and made him look. The man watched the frail, mutilated body of the girl. Her flesh was torn as if for sport and left hanging as if she were a victim of a threshing machine. Hutton vomited loudly.

Bolan held the two men in his gaze. "This is what I'm fighting. What I live with and fight against every day. And there are hundreds more just like me who are going to have to live with this for the rest of their lives. So take your cute phrases and bury them somewhere. Until you can understand the reality of this war, you can stay behind with the rear echelons."

Hutton still retched with heaving slowness. Edelman was green but did not give way. Evidently he had some self-control, more than most new recruits, Bolan gave him that. The private resumed disposal, and Bolan went back to Crawford's office.

The major was angry at Bolan's insubordination. But Crawford knew the sergeant and what he was up against. To Bolan, who practically lived in enemy territory, everybody was Rear.

"Sergeant, just who the hell do you think you are? You—"

Bolan cut the major off. The big soldier was dirty, tired, and had a Communist porter's blood all down his shirtfront. "With all due respect, sir. I've read Hutton's stuff, and he can't see anything but one story: Ugly Americans Murder Innocents. And Edelman. . .Edelman hasn't said much one way or the other. If you want PR, get a journalist who's grown up in a war and not on a college campus. Sir."

The major paused. Something in the penetrator's hollow eyes made him listen.

Crawford spoke up. "Major, the sergeant has a point, but there's no reason not to let Hutton go along on the evacuation. The soldiers are going through the villages to clear the people for their own safety. Hutton can't see anything wrong in that."

The major considered the point. "Colonel, I think you're right. We need the people at home to start backing this war. That means PR. And if this evac isn't good publicity, I don't know what is. Hutton is going to cover the evacuation. As for Edelman accompanying the sergeant here, I think we should leave that up to the sergeant. Journalists don't fit in on penetration missions. He could get killed." The major made to depart, but pausing in the doorway, he added, "I've got to admit, though, I never met a journalist who was worth keeping."

BOLAN PACKED for his final mission into the Steel Circle. Magazines, bayonet, and claymores with blasting wire and a clacker--the trigger mechanism for the mechanical ambush— all went into his rucksack. But first everything had to be cleaned. One piece of dirt could mean the difference between survival and death. He was not confused about which one he wanted.

A figure entered the hooch. It was Edelman.

"Sergeant."

"Edelman."

"I'd like to come with you on your mission and get your side of the story."

Bolan looked at the correspondent. The shock therapy had

worked. The man was beginning to see that just maybe there were some things a writer back home didn't know about. Maybe Bolan could cover the guy's ass long enough for him to learn something. Bolan paused.

"All right. For once I'm going to take a scribbler along with me. But remember, the mission comes first and your safety comes second. Understand?"

Edelman nodded. "I signed a waiver to that effect."

THEY DROVE OUT OF CAMP under an ominous sky. The cloud banks had continued to mount through the afternoon and were now piled into angry mountains of gray and black. As the jeep bounced over the rutted track, the setting sun slipped under the cloud cover and shone on the underside of the clouds, turning them into a rolling ceiling of blood.

The comparative safety that made the camp feel a little like home was quickly left behind. Still, it might have been Louisiana they were driving through except that they were halfway around the world in a thankless war that was as hard on the survivors as it was on the casualties. The dense wall of greenery on either side of the road rushed by in forbidding anonymity. The jungle was still and silent under the threat of the storm. The humidity was palpable.

"Are we out of camp, Edelman?"

Edelman shot one of his keen glances at Bolan. Obviously Bolan wasn't just asking about a fact. The big sergeant had been putting his mind along a forced march through hard reality and he did not know where this question might lead.

"We're out of camp, Edelman. There are no commanding officers here, no editors, no regulations. Take off the civilian clothes. If you're coming then you're coming all the way." Bolan reached into the back of the jeep and grabbed a pair of infantry fatigues. He threw them to his companion.

Bolan stopped the jeep. The journalist jumped out and

stripped and then climbed back in. He got dressed like a soldier as Bolan drove on. Then the sergeant reached behind him again and threw something to Edelman.

A .45 Colt Commander landed in his lap. "That's for you," said Bolan. "Ever used one?" Edelman was holding it gingerly, considering whether or not he should accept it.

"I'm a writer, Sergeant. I just observe."

Edelman looked at Bolan, but the soldier kept his eyes on the road. "There is no such thing as an observer in this world," Bolan said. "Those who think they are observers have copped out. Your camera is an observer. *You* are a man. Take responsibility for your actions."

Edelman was still turning the gun over. He knew the big sergeant was purposely breaking him down. But knowing it didn't help.

"Say we're out on the mission," Bolan went on. "I'm tied up with a squad of Charlie spitting heavy lead. A family of villagers is running away from the firefight. Okay so far?" Edelman nodded. "One of the VC throws a grenade, and it lands right beside a woman running with her baby. Hutton, if he wasn't covering his ass, would take a picture of them. Award for excellence in journalism." Bolan paused. "What about you?"

"I might die," Edelman said truthfully.

Bolan reached back once more and threw Edelman an extra clip for the Colt.

"Here. You said you signed a waiver for your personal safety, didn't you?"

WHEN NIGHT FELL Bolan took the jeep off the road and hid it in a small gully. Edelman watched closely as Bolan brushed away the tire tracks and covered the vehicle with foliage. Before they started off, the soldier brought Edelman closer and said softly, "We're going to move now." The whisper, sounding eerie in

the stillness, sent a chill down the journalist's spine. "Do no
make a sound. Keep your hand on the back of my ruck or you'l
lose me. Say nothing until I tell you to. If you have any
questions, save them until we get back to camp."

That was it. Instantly they were moving, Edelman holding
the back of Bolan's ruck. The march quickly became a night
mare for him. He was acutely aware of his own helplessness
All he could see was blackness. Leaves brushed his face like the
clutching fingers of the Vietcong. Overhead a canopy of foliage
blocked out the sky. Once, Edelman thought he smelled a
rotting animal.

It was like walking blindfolded straight into the belly of hell
And yet this soldier in front of him managed to slip silently
along the invisible trail as if he knew where every leaf and
every protruding root would be.

They stopped after twenty minutes for Edelman to rest and
catch his breath. He badly wanted to speak to the sergeant, to
hear the reassurance of his voice in this black pit, but the man
was keeping to his own thoughts.

Back in Crawford's hut there was something about Bolan that
had shocked Edelman. Now Edelman knew that whatever it
was that had shocked him about the soldier was what was
necessary for survival in this tropical hell. He did not have a
name for it.

After what seemed an eternity of humping through the bush
Bolan stopped. He reached down and picked a long blade of
grass and placed it in his teeth. Then he lowered himself to the
ground and slithered slowly forward.

Edelman was swept by a wave of doubt. Was this what had
shocked him? Was the soldier completely out of his mind? Had
the war done it to him? Was he now just going to slither off into
the night like a giant reptile?

He heard Bolan's whisper. "In the middle of this path is a thin
wire about four inches off the ground. VC booby trap. I'm

going to lead you over it." They moved across the place that Bolan somehow knew was a trail.

About a hundred yards in from the track they set up on a small knoll at the base of a tree. Bolan rummaged silently in his ruck and handed Edelman a Starlite scope. Edelman looked through the eyepiece as Bolan whispered.

"Fifteen yards down there's a cart track. See it? Coolies use it to transport arms and ammunition to the local VC cells. There are routes like that one all over the place." Edelman saw something move. Silently he handed the scope to Bolan. The sergeant looked through it and then handed it back. "See that pair of coolies? Look at the one on the right. Those things slung on his shoulder are AK-47s. He's got them padded with cloth so they don't rattle. The other one's got a cart. Probably loaded with ammo or mortar rounds." Edelman felt his heart pounding; he had never been so close to the enemy. Glancing at Bolan he could tell that the sergeant was at home.

"The cells around here are led by a guerilla called the Green Dragon. Those porters are going to lead us to the cell they're supplying, but I don't think to the Dragon himself. Keep alert. We're moving double-time."

Bolan took the scope and was suddenly moving again. Edelman scrambled up and found the back of the sergeant's ruck. They trotted through the jungle parallel to the trail.

Bolan was taking them over every obstacle because the VC mined the easy routes. Edelman had known that before, but the reality that a mine could explode and make him a corpse or a cripple made him shudder.

Bolan pushed Edelman down and thrust the scope into his hands. He showed the newsman where a squad of VC stood, AKs ready: the rendezvous.

"I'm going to hit them. Stay here and keep your eyes open. I'll come back and get you."

Then he was gone.

Terror gripped the journalist like a giant icy hand. What if Bolan didn't return . . . ? It didn't bear thinking about. He knew nothing about the jungle or about combat. He was completely helpless. No, not completely. He pulled the Colt out of his belt. Suddenly he was grinning wryly; according to the rules he was now a combatant. Now the VC could kill him legally; before, they could only have murdered him.

BOLAN MOVED PARALLEL to the trail. He knew where it led, but it was sure to be guarded ahead of the rendezvous point. He circled downwind. Killing the group of VC huddled in the clearing would not be very difficult. A couple of frags and the M-16 would do it. But the guards spread around the perimeter could present a problem.

He was going to make it just a little safer.

He crouched in the jungle about twenty yards from the edge of the clearing, waiting for the coolies to arrive. The guards would get nervous right about then because someone had been following porters and sniping them to pieces. Soft voices drifted in from the clearing. They had arrived.

A small click sounded to his left as a guard put his weapon on automatic.

Bolan circled the guard's position like a formless shadow. The sergeant had a special technique for killing sentries without making a sound.

He waited until he could make out the man lying in a small depression with his weapon resting on the berm.

Bolan was so close he could hear the VC lookout breathe. Then Bolan moved. One foot jammed the weapon against the ground, snapping the watch's trigger finger. At the same time he slit the VC's throat. A slight bubbling sound came from the guerrilla's windpipe as Bolan slipped the knife between his ribs and cut his heart in two. The VC would make no half-dead movements to give him away.

Bolan knew the habits of the VC. They always set up the same way around a rendezvous and Bolan knew approximately where the next perimeter sentry would be. Again he waited in the bush. The voices in the clearing continued speaking softly.

It was only a small sound, an AK butt scraping the dirt. But it was all Bolan needed.

Two more sounds joined the first as Bolan sent the guard into the void: his trigger finger snapping, and a muted gasp. Bolan picked up the body and carried it toward the VC in the clearing.

At the edge of the site, ten yards from the VC squad, Bolan lowered the corpse. He was going to be so close to the VC when he fragged them he would need the cover of the lifeless form. He crouched behind the guard's chest and pulled three frags from his belt. He jerked the pins quickly and sent the grenades spinning into the knot of Cong.

The blast lit the jungle night and sent a shock wave slamming into his unlikely protection. In an instant Bolan was up firing, the M-16 on full-auto. He sent spurts of 5.56mm death into anything that moved. He ran one way and then the other.

The perimeter guards opened up from the wall of growth. Bolan inserted a full mag as they blasted the spot he had been standing in a second before. He emptied the mag into the clearing, then melted into the jungle.

Seconds later Edelman felt the soldier at his side. The writer stuck the Colt back into his belt. They both ran back the way they had come. Edelman smacked full face into Bolan's ruck as the sergeant stopped suddenly in his tracks. The booby trap again. Edelman crossed it, wanting to run as fast as his legs would carry him. The surviving VC were coming after them.

The sergeant bent down, groaning loudly. Was he hit? With relief and sudden understanding Edelman saw that the soldier was fiddling with the trip wire. The guards came through the jungle now heading directly toward them. Bolan groaned again.

They slipped into the long grass and waited for the guards to catch up. Bolan held a thin monofilament line that he had tied to the trip wire of the booby trap.

The guards came along the trail, trying to follow quietly. They slowed down as they crossed the wire. Then Bolan jerked the line. The exploding mines shredded the VC guards. Edelman felt a piece of wet meat splatter onto his forehead. Then they were up and moving.

DAWN STREAKED THE HORIZON in oyster-yellow as Bolan and Edelman drove back to camp.

The threatening storm had suddenly let go and drenched them during the long hump back to the jeep. The trail had turned into a black quagmire of ooze that stuck to their boots and made the journey twice as long, twice as miserable.

Edelman was deep in thought. He had never wanted to be that close to killing. The scene was etched into his mind like a horror movie he was forced to watch over and over again. He was tired, cramped and cold. The rain had washed them clean of the blood and mine-sprayed gore, but to Edelman it seemed that it stuck to him right through to his soul.

Bolan drove in stony silence.

The only time Edelman spoke was at first light.

"Do you like to kill, Sergeant?"

Bolan turned and looked at him with hollow eyes.

"That's the wrong question," he said, as if he had been expecting it. Then he lapsed into silence.

The gate to the camp was guarded by MPs instead of soldiers. Bolan braked, identified himself and Edelman, and was directed into the camp.

"Confined to base, soldier," said an MP. "You're staying here."

"What's this all about?" asked Edelman. For once Bolan did not know. MPs were all over the place. One shack was heavily guarded. Hutton was walking around accosting soldiers but none would talk to him. Bolan left Edelman and reported to Crawford.

He did not need to ask. Crawford looked worried. His eyes were ringed with gray. "Nguyen took Hutton along yesterday afternoon to follow Nile Barrabas's group clearing the villages. When they got to Hoi Binh, they found the whole village massacred—men, women and children. Forty of 'em, hacked to pieces, Mack. Barrabas had already left. Only survivor was an old man who kept mumbling about the American patrol murdering everyone.

"Hutton went mad taking pictures of everything. Used up every roll of film he had. Says this is the biggest Vietnam story ever to hit the wire."

"What did Barrabas say?"

"Denied it. Said they left the villagers packing and went on to Ap Quan."

"So what's going on?"

"Pentagon East is sending in an inquiry officer to investigate. We're under confinement and being replaced by another battalion tomorrow or the next day. It really hit the fan this time, Mack."

Bolan was enraged.

"You don't believe Barrabas would do that, do you? I've seen him risk his life a hundred times for villagers. Done it with him. Barrabas wouldn't do that, and you and I both know it."

Crawford shrugged. "It's out of my hands, Mack."

"And another thing," said Bolan. "All it takes is a day or two for Charlie to move into the Steel Circle and dig in. Free-fire zone or not, this will all have been for nothing. The night will really belong to Charlie."

Crawford looked at the big guy. Bolan was usually cool but the injustice had raised his fury.

Bolan was thinking fast now, desperately searching for a solution. "Where's Nguyen? I want to talk to him."

"Can't find him. Brought Hutton back to base and hung around for a while, but I can't find him now."

They paused. Crawford caught the drift of the sergeant's thinking. There was an MP standing five feet away, and they could not say what they were both planning.

"Soldier," Crawford said to the MP. "Sergeant Bolan has been humping patrols every night for two weeks, and I want him to rest. Keep that asshole Hutton away from his hut. And that goes for your men, too, at least until tomorrow morning. He needs a good night's rest."

The MP looked at Bolan's combat-smeared fatigues and nodded. To him the boonierat sniper was obviously on the edge of what military psychologists termed Acute Environmental Reaction. Enlisted men called it going batshit. Shows in the eyes. This one was a dead ringer.

Bolan tromped off to his hut, deep in thought. The whole thing stank. Bolan was going to get Nguyen and find out why.

And he'd better have the right answers or the little guide would regret he was ever born.

A HUSH PERMEATED THE CAMP. Bolan surveyed the quiet midday scene from his hut while the soldiers played poker in glum silence. Four MPs guarded the gate. Another three stood outside the hut where Barrabas was held. The rest patrolled the perimeter. Bolan knew what Barrabas was up against. The two men had fought together in the worst actions and their respect and trust went deep.

He pictured the helpless Nile, facing a lifetime of shame and disgrace for something he had not done. A conviction for an atrocity like that would be the end of Barrabas. Throw away one good life. "I'm not going to let that happen, Nile," Bolan whispered to himself.

Yeah, he would do it for Nile. In the larger sense he was doing it for the villagers at Hoi Binh. Innocent people, used brutally in the evil drive for power and domination that fed the enemies of Bolan.

He slipped from the hut like a wraith.

The sentries had little to guard; the camp was surrounded by inhospitable jungle and primitive villages. Following news of the massacre, the one nearby town would be no haven. The soldiers were not going anywhere, but Bolan was. He picked his moment and made the fence, then vanished into the jungle.

From the ordnance in his own billet the big guy had armed himself for a one-man blitz. It was a surprising array of munitions: claymores; C-4 explosive compound with blasting caps and firing batteries; monofilament line and trigger mechanisms; canteens filled with gasoline; M-16 rifle with extra magazines; Colt Commander; bayonet, steel spike and frags.

He had never trusted Nguyen. The noncom with the Popular Forces had always seemed to hold himself aloof from the operations. Bolan was more aware than most Americans of the cultural differences between Asians and Westerners, but in this case he distinguished between inscrutability and plain shiftiness. Nguyen always landed on the ineffective side of operations, never getting caught in a VC ambush. No suspicion attached to any specific incident but together it all added up.

Bolan headed for the town of Mu Son, where he knew Nguyen spent some of his off-duty hours. Moving quickly on a bush trail, he covered the distance in just over an hour.

Mu Son was a typical Vietnamese town, essentially Asian but with odd reminders of the French colonial regime. Bicycles and pushcarts milled through the streets past shops and shanties, moving noisily around ancient Citroën sedans.

The women wore sheath dresses and silk trousers, the men baggy black pants and loose-fitting long shirts. Children were everywhere. Bolan stashed his gear beside an old ramshackle railway station and headed for the bar that Nguyen frequented. He kept his steel spike close at hand, hidden up his sleeve.

News of the massacre had spread and Bolan was toying with fate just showing his American face. It would be impossible for the tall, two-hundred-plus-pound infantryman to be inconspicuous on the streets of an Asian town where the average male was five foot three. He had no choice but to walk openly and quickly down the side streets and alleys to the bar.

He left the brilliant afternoon sunlight and entered the gloom of the dingy watering hole. Tinny music came from a transistor radio. Two Vietnamese girls sat at the end of the bar with no-tea-no-talk-no-money-no-honey faces turned to the big sergeant. The bartender sat smoking. Bolan headed straight for him.

"I'm looking for Nguyen Tan."

The man stared at him and continued to smoke, then put the cigarette out carefully.

"Not here."

"I have to find him. Where does his family live? His girlfriend?"

The barman launched into a rapid set of complicated directions, half Vietnamese, half English. Bolan followed it, comparing it to his mental map, and realized the man was sending him on a wild-goose chase.

He reached over and grabbed the little man by the shirtfront, lifting him over the counter with one arm. He carried him out the back door into an alley of dried mud, garbage and dog droppings. The big American forced the Vietnamese to the ground, then sat on his torso. The little man wheezed with the weight of the sergeant on his lungs. Bolan pressed the steel spike against one eyelid.

"Now, I know you can speak English better than that, my friend. You're going to tell me where to find Nguyen Tan, and it better be right."

Bolan tangled his fingers in the man's hair. Slowly the spike came down until the point formed a dimple in the little bar-keeper's eyelid. The man flinched, trying to somehow hide his head in the dirt. Then the guy spoke in rapid bursts, fighting the crushing weight on his chest.

"Nguyen's girlfriend, name Brigitte Bardot. Beside post office. Back door."

Bolan stood up. The diminutive Oriental scrambled to his feet, checking his eye for blood.

Bolan moved fast.

The woman's house was a dilapidated shack. He walked through the thin door as if it didn't exist and brought his face right up to hers. She was small and slight. Bolan dwarfed her small abode. Panic gripped her as the big soldier looked into her with his hollow death eyes.

"I want Nguyen."

He left it at that. She knew what was in store for her.

"Not here," she said in a tight, quavering voice.

"I want him, understand?" Bolan's face was within two inches of hers. His hands twitched: once, twice....

The woman gave way to her rising terror and panic.

"They will kill you, bastard," she flung at him, recoiling from his big hard body. "Nguyen and his brother will take Steel Circle! All you American soldier die or go back where you came from. We will crush running dogs of imperialism," she recited.

"His brother?"

"Green Dragon," she boasted spitefully. "Greatest guerrilla fighter Vietcong ever see. They come for all of you. We will have victory."

That was all Bolan needed to know. Nguyen was the Green Dragon's brother. That explained how the VC managed to stay one step ahead of the American grunts, how they struck so hard in just the right places and then disappeared.

The VC had massacred the villagers at Hoi Binh. Nguyen had led Hutton right into it, knowing the American forces would be tied up for days with the scandal. Yeah, the VC were moving in and installing themselves in the Steel Circle, digging in.

Like hell they were.

Bolan was going hunting. Little Nguyen would confess if it was the last thing the treacherous guide ever did.

Bolan left the woman sobbing in the shack. As he came around to the front of the building an MP patrol drove past. Bolan ducked back, then peered around the corner and watched as the MPs left the jeep in the street and went into a building. Bolan walked up and got into the vehicle as if he owned it.

Bolan soon left the town behind and was flying down the dirt road past rice fields where farmers plowed with water buffalo. He swerved to avoid peasants carrying loads on shoulder yokes, past the rickety train tracks and toward the jungle. He had one more mission into the Steel Circle: find the VC. Find the Green Dragon. Find Nguyen.

The road became an overgrown track hung with branches and vines. Overhead the foliage had merged into a thick canopy. The place was damp with the afternoon humidity. It was like driving into a dark tunnel. He could feel the jungle surrounding him.

A bullet whizzed past his ear. Bolan rolled from the jeep and let it run into the dense tangle of undergrowth. He heard the engine stall. He waited, tensed to spring.

He knew the VC's mind like he knew his own. Snipe. Then wait. Watch. Make sure they are dead. Then take what intelligence you can from the scene and leave.

Slowly he eased away from the road into the bush. The sniper would wait in the growth on the other side, watching.

Bolan headed back the way he had come. Fifty yards up the road he crossed to the other side. Bolan willed himself toward the faceless enemy. To remain utterly silent through the jungle took infinite patience. The ambusher would wait another ten minutes before he was sure the kill was true. Bolan spent almost that long coming back down the fifty yards, watching every bush, every shadow.

The sniper thought he had a big kill. The jeep had seemed too good to be true. He was waiting just up from the jeep, five yards back into the jungle. Bolan watched the guy's back. The American slithered toward the sniper, knife in hand. One snapping twig would send the guy whirling around to blow Bolan apart.

The VC tensed as Bolan crept within ten feet of him. The man sensed that somebody was close and began to turn his head.

Too late. Bolan lunged across the last ten feet. One hand brought the knife to the enemy's throat, the other imprisoning his weapon arm. Dark, terror-filled eyes strained up in their sockets as Bolan pulled him farther back into the jungle.

Bolan went down on one knee. He positioned the man with the small of his back resting on the raised knee. Press with one hand on the neck and the other below the belt. Bolan pressed down.

"I not afraid to die," gasped the VC.

Bolan had learned a little of the language himself.

"What if I just break your back and leave you in the jungle here? How many days would it take for you to die? Six? Ten?" He paused and increased the pressure until the spine was about to snap. "I'll leave you here with nothing to help you kill yourself." The VC hung there, straining against the relentless pressure.

"What do you want?" he choked out.

"Nguyen Tan. Tell me now or I'll leave you to the leeches."

He told Bolan where to find the VC camp. Bolan jammed the steel spike into the corner of the sniper's eye and through into his brain. One less.

Bolan returned to the jeep. The dense jungle had stopped the vehicle without damaging it. Bolan reversed onto the road and headed deeper into the Circle. Now for Nguyen. The little guide had pretended shock when he heard of the Hoi Binh massacre. He'd be really shocked when Bolan caught up with him.

EDELMAN WAS BEGINNING TO UNDERSTAND. He had asked the big soldier if he enjoyed killing, and the sergeant told him "wrong question." In the hours back at camp the writer had figured it out.

No, the soldier did not get a thrill from killing. If he lusted for anything, it was justice, not blood. He just did what he had to do. Right now that meant fighting the atrocities that shocked people like Edelman. Later, the sergeant would have something else to fight.

Edelman had always thought himself a good person. He did not hurt people, he believed in freedom and he was always prepared to write a story that would shake people up if the story needed to be written. The Vietnam War, and the big sergeant in particular, had shown him that he had to do more. Edelman's ideals did not mean a jot in the whirling vortex of unfolding events.

The writer was finally facing it: the world did not care what people with good intentions wished. The world was full of evil men doing evil things to satisfy their misguided urges. Bolan was one of the few going up against them.

The question was not "do you enjoy killing?" It was "when will it end?" And Edelman knew the answer to that one.

Never.

DUSK WAS FALLING on the Green Dragon's camp, turning the whole scene a half-light gray. Shadows merged to create indistinct forms. Bolan circled the camp, invisible. Fifty Vietcong fighters waited a few yards away. They wanted to move out and kill. The jungle breathed like a waiting animal.

They were armed with ComBloc weapons. Few of them were

in the shelters. They were waiting for it to get dark enough before moving out on their mission. The Steel Circle was theirs, they chuckled among themselves. The Americans were caught and they were going to drive them into shame.

Mack Bolan was no longer a man. Eternities in the jungle on lonely sniping missions had dulled the distinction between himself and this leafy world. He knew now that the green hell was not a jumble of separate plants and animals, and that he was not a separate being. He was a part of it, and it was a part of him.

When it twitched, he jerked. Call it refined awareness, call it ESP. He did not call it anything. He just used it to locate VC guards that were so well hidden they could not be seen. But he could feel one now.

And he was training a gun on Bolan's head.

Bolan melted back into the bush and circled around the sentry's position.

In the Vietnamese jungle one man could stand quietly and yet be heard, while another could walk five feet away and you would never know he was there.

Like Bolan. He was close enough to see the enemy's veins throbbing in his neck. The VC fighter was tense, searching the undergrowth for whatever it was he had seen.

Bolan executed his stomp-and-slice technique. A wheeze and dribble, and another life from the wrong side was sent into the void. Bolan wiped his blade on the VC's uniform.

Next, said Bolan's mind to the jungle. It answered with a muffled cough, allowing Bolan to pinpoint the location of another lookout.

He found the guard with his AK across his knees. The guard was holding the firing mechanism of a captured American claymore. The device could blast a deadly spray of tiny steel balls into an approaching enemy. Bolan decided to use some of the VC's own medicine on them. Using the grayness of the dusk and the foliage as an ally, he searched for the claymore itself, following the wires with his eyes.

He located the claymore, some distance to the rear of the sentry, and began to work on it. Bolan loosened the device and slowly rotated it until it pointed toward the sentry. The first firefight would cause the guard to blow the claymore into his own face.

Bolan slipped back and headed past the dead VC, looking for the next one. He needed room to work. A minute later, another pounding enemy heart was sliced cleanly in two.

Bolan worked quietly, he was now within earshot of the VC milling about in the camp. He could hear the metallic sounds as a few cleaned their weapons. Others were discussing torture techniques.

Bolan was setting up a one-man combat assault. He moved about the section of the unguarded perimeter. In the crooks of small trees he set up magazines of 5.56mm rounds and attached shavings of C-4 explosive to them, firmly wedging the whole device down. With six of these "soldiers" spread out along the perimeter, he had a squad of infantry. He spaced out his claymores between the trees and to either side, wiring them to the detonating battery. The rest of the C-4 he set up at the edge of the clearing.

With the canteens he silently laid a tiny trail of gasoline from tree to tree and up to the C-4 under the mags. The rest he spread in a line parallel to the perimeter.

Guards broke away to spell those on duty. Seeing his relief approaching, the sentry with the claymore rose. They were both standing there talking when the others found they were relieving dead men. Spooked by the shout that went up, the VC fired the claymore, turning himself and his replacement into a grisly, reeling mess as the steel balls ripped through them.

The camp was in an uproar. VC rushed in the direction of the blast, firing into the jungle. Bolan blew his seven claymores and took eight VC out of action in a percussive smash of fury. He lit the gasoline, sending fire running through the jungle. The C-4 shreds flared into white-hot flame igniting the squad of magazines. Red-orange tracers began whipping through the camp in a barrage of death.

The VC fired into the jungle where the squad of imperialist dogs were attacking. They fired and then rushed forward. Bolan blew the C-4. It shot a roiling flame of explosion into the rushing VC bodies. Six more gone. Screams arose from the wounded.

Bolan had to get to the other side of the camp before the squad of magazines ran out. He raced around, making as much noise as he could in the midst of the hell screams. The VC were rushing around in disarray, firing at phantoms that blew them apart in the wild firefight, and throwing grenades helter-skelter in their fear.

Bolan cruised in from behind, picking them off with the M-16. None of them could have noticed without eyes in the back of their head. Which they got, spewing blood.

He moved and reacted instinctively, too fast for normal thought. Two VC came out of a tent. One was Nguyen, who saw the big guy and rushed him. The other was the Green Dragon, who marshaled his men.

Bolan met Nguyen's charge and smashed the pistol from his hand. With adrenaline-spurred fury Bolan grabbed the guide and jammed the Colt under his chin, the muzzle pointing up into Nguyen's treacherous brain. With the other hand he kept stroking the M-16's trigger, blasting the VC. They began moving back into the jungle.

The 5.56 mags ran out. In the sudden quiet the screams of the wounded took on the pitch of police sirens at a riot.

But two dozen VC still stood, now led by the Green Dragon. They spotted the American dragging Nguyen from the camp. Bolan's eyes locked with the Green Dragon's.

Yeah, he was a leader all right. Bolan saw it in the way the man moved: no hesitation, just control. He was all hard muscles under a fading uniform with eyes that matched Bolan's in coldness. This was the one that Bolan had hunted for on so many night missions. This was the elusive monster.

His eyes still locked with Bolan's, the Green Dragon hissed orders to his men to flank the American but to hold their fire.

Bolan kept backing out of the camp.

At the edge of the jungle Bolan forced Nguyen into a crouch. Then, as if with reckless abandonment, he rose up with the struggling Nguyen, exposing them both to fire. The Green Dragon looked at him in surprise for one split second too long. Bolan had already raised the M-16 and put a burst through the Green Dragon's face.

Bolan swung around, jerking the little guide to his feet and forced him to run toward the jeep.

The VC crashed through the jungle after them, leaving their leader's body twitching with only a 5.56mm-chopped pulp atop the shoulders. They would have to catch right up to get a shot at Bolan without risk of hitting Nguyen. Bolan kept the guide running. He had left the vehicle in a dry riverbed about a hundred yards away. It came in sight with the VC only twenty yards behind.

Bolan slammed the guide into the vehicle, fired a quick burst, sending the VC diving for cover. He handcuffed Nguyen to the post under the seat. With Nguyen yelling at the top of his lungs and the VC rushing again, the engine roared into life. Bolan sent a spray of humus down the riverbed as the jeep shot forward. Shots ricocheted off the jeep with a multiple clang as the big guy took it around a bend in the dry watercourse and flung it up the side. The vehicle lurched onto the track in a four-wheel frenzy. A VC grenade sent it bucking but failed to stop the escape.

Ten minutes later Bolan stopped. He took off the handcuffs,

which had ripped mercilessly at the guide's wrists during the
bumpy ride, and replaced them with something far more dangerous. A minute later Nguyen was sitting upright in the seat,
the butt of the M-16 jammed into his crotch and the muzzle
poking up into the underside of his jaw. He was securely tied
with the last knot around the M-16's trigger.

"One wrong move, Nguyen, and you're going to blow your
own head off."

It was not that Bolan took any pleasure in inflicting pain or
being cruel. He did what needed to be done. Right now that
meant preparing Nguyen for his confession back at camp.
Bolan had moved the rifle's select lever to "safe" without
Nguyen knowing.

Bolan drove over the rutted track.

"Feeling a little bumpy, huh?"

Nguyen's eyes rolled in terror.

"Maybe I should just hit that pothole over there and let you
have a little accident before we get back."

THE INQUIRY OFFICER had arrived and was interviewing Crawford in the command hut when Bolan pulled into camp. Nguyen
had to be led into the office with an MP on either arm. His pants
were soaked. Bolan was also escorted since he was under arrest
for leaving without permission and for stealing the jeep.

"I've got the star witness right here, sir," Bolan said to the
inquiry officer. "He's ready to talk and you'll save yourself a
lot of trouble." Crawford's relief was evident. His gamble in
letting Bolan go had paid off.

Bolan remained under arrest and waited outside while the
inquiry officer interviewed the demoralized guide in the command hut. The jeep would take some explaining. Crawford
would see to that.

After an hour of "persuasion," the investigation's officer
emerged from the hut, ordered Nguyen held for treason and

then relieved the MPs of their assignment at the camp. An official exoneration would follow.

The big Nile Barrabas stepped out of the hut where he had been held. Crawford briefed him on Bolan's one-man mission. The captain beamed his gratitude as he strode up to shake the sergeant's blood-crusted hand. They said little. Another notch of respect went into their friendship.

Bolan was not interested in being a hero. He tromped wearily back to his hut, exhausted.

Hutton was desolate. The journalistic coup he had held in his hands had dissolved into nothing. He shrank from the big soldier's hollow death eyes.

Bolan did not bother to rub Hutton's face in it. He had learned long before that just as there were some things worth risking his life for, there were others that did not deserve a second glance. Hutton was one of them.

Edelman stood between Bolan and his hooch.

"I'm going to write about it, Sergeant. I know what you're fighting, and I'm going to make sure people find out. Watch for my name."

Bolan nodded. Edelman had been worth the effort. It meant one writer who would tell the truth. One who would start showing people the world for what it really was. It was up to the readers to take it from there. Yeah, Edelman was worth keeping.

Dark thunderheads had built up again over the piedmont. They piled higher and higher until the sky was a massive black fist of storm. Peals of thunder mixed with the sounds of artillery as the big guns began to pound the Steel Circle. Don Edelman watched as the weary soldier climbed into his hut.

It had been one hell of a day and night for the writer.

With one hell of a flash of truth.

And now, for him, the big war had just begun.

Laser Raze

"Son of a bitch," said the American general.

It was the fourth day of the Feria del San Fermin, the festival of the running of the bulls in Pamplona, Spain. The general and his young girlfriend were drinking tintos in a café across the square from the statue of Ernest Hemingway. The general was an old man reliving his youth in the company of a beautiful woman.

He was allowed.

His wife of thirty-seven years had died eight months before. He'd loved that woman, and the winter in Madrid had tested him to find new reasons for staying alive. Finally, Albierto Manez, King Juan Carlos's aide, had knowingly introduced the general to a woman who was the spitting image of the Margaret of his youth.

Angela was beautiful. She made General George Armstrong West feel as strong as he'd felt when he was a pup, fighting Franco's Republicans in the golden years when there was only one evil in the world and its name was fascism.

Now he courted Angela in a high style that he hoped would make up for the great difference in their ages.

The general knew women. To delight Angela, he had added an element of mystery to each rendezvous with her. Recently a car was sent for her. It took her to a waiting plane. The plane took her to an island. On the island a helicopter lifted her to a pavilion in the mountains. The general greeted her from the pavilion with the offer of a horse ride along the ridges of the Canaries before dinner. They rode to where a group of islanders spoke to each other in whistle-language across a great valley.

In one of the canyons, the general had dinner waiting. They ate with the islanders. Angela had the bright glow of a woman who'd fallen deeply in love. And in the morning the general whispered into his shaving mirror, "George, you're pretty smart for an old bastard."

HE STARED AT THE THREE MEN holding Kalashnikovs who had stepped out of a black panel van moments before. The men spread out and moved toward the café. "Son of a bitch," he said. "Angela, get your pretty duff off to the powder room. I've got business."

The three men spread out to cover the exits of the café. The general observed them. He felt a tap on his shoulder. "Your woman got away, General. If you will now come with me there will be no trouble." West turned to see an old-style Tokarev TT 33 pointed at his face.

"BNF?" he asked quickly. The dark-haired man holding the weapon nodded yes. A cold chill ran down West's spine. His memory flashed to a Madrid street only a few years before. The American admiral's car had been bombed and West had been one of the first to visit the scene. Evidently the Basque Nation and Freedom group had mined the entire street, had probably been planning the operation for years in advance. In a hidden courtyard of the devastated street, the general had looked up to see the admiral's twisted limousine embedded in the second story balcony of the house. "This is it," he'd told himself, shocked to the core at the sight. "This is the new war for the next generation of young men."

He couldn't understand it then, and, as he left the café under guard, he realized he had no idea how to fight it now.

THE GENERAL CAME TO in the same dark cell where Justo, the BNF chief, had first led him. Pain spread over his torso in small waves that crashed on his diaphragm.

He shifted onto his left side and grunted at a new kind of pain. His arms had been handcuffed tightly behind him and his shoulders ached from the interrogation officer's blows.

The man was clearly KGB—West recognized the type. The slick Western suits and the well-fed body disciplined by mandatory sessions in Moscow's Dynamo Training Club were trademarks of Russian intelligence officers in the 1980s. The man's educated English and his sadistic arrogance were KGB trademarks, too.

West was surprised that a Russian worked directly with the BNF. He knew the Basques were Marxist, but intelligence insisted that, with the exception of an ammunition and training exchange with the IRA, the Basques pretty much ran their own show. Stakes must be getting higher, he realized.

West knew what information the Russian wanted, but he had never anticipated it was so vital that the KGB would risk kidnapping a U.S. general.

When he heard the footsteps coming toward his door, George Armstrong West reminded himself that the only way to prolong his life was to tough it out. Until they had the intel they wanted, West would stay alive.

And the longer he stayed alive, the greater the chance that something worthwhile would come of his promised meeting with Mack Bolan in Pamplona. He was not able to make the meeting, of course, but Bolan most certainly would.

The trouble was, old men have a bad habit of dying during interrogation. So he thought of Angela, and how she made him feel young again, and he decided that when things got really rough he would think some more of Angela.

THE INTERROGATION ROOM was an eyeless cinder-block box

that West assumed was in the basement of the same building as his cell. He sat bound in a chair that was bolted to the floor. Justo and the Russian were standing apart, far apart, he noted.

Justo tried the nice-guy approach on him. "Look, General," he said, "you know we are professionals. You are professional, too. Make it easy on yourself. Give us what we need, then we can all relax and wait for Juan Carlos's government to release the prisoners. Once the ransom is met, you're a free man. You can go back to your beautiful woman. Simple, no?"

"What prisoners?" West asked, not looking at the terrorist.

This time the Russian spoke. "You're a valuable man, General. You were a Communist once, yes?"

"Communist, hell," shouted West. "I was a young kid fighting Franco. Franco was a Nazi, remember? Nobody likes Nazis."

"We need your information, General," the Russian said, ignoring his outburst. "Tell us first, for example, exactly when the United States plans to begin the naval base for which you are now negotiating with Spain."

"That's a lot of crap," the general said.

"We would like to know everything, General," the Russian continued. "Begin by outlining the strategic profile for the base that will be built in Ceuta—what you Americans call Spanish Morocco."

"Persuade me," West said.

THE GENERAL CAME TO AGAIN feeling as old and as afflicted as Job. It had been a bad session. Stok, the name Justo had called the KGB man, administered the beating personally and scientifically, and when he sensed the old man might die on him, he had terminated the session. West could not remember being returned to the cell. How much more could his fast-aging body stand?

Now he lay facedown on the cot in the darkened room. No

cuffs on him this time. He tried to lift himself from the mattress and felt the pain in his arms where Stok had stunned him repeatedly with the cattle prod.

He fell forward on the bed, and his weight pushed his face deep into the mattress. Jesus, I could smother here, he thought, too old and too weak to lift my own weight.

What kept him going through these indignities was not, he knew, the old mule-hard fight that had seen him through every major conflict since the Spanish Civil War. That fight was gone. He struggled to get up from the mattress because of Angela. He did not want her to read about an old man who was too weak, too broken to carry his own weight.

When at last the general sat up he felt a new spear of pain in his left side. Exploring it with a shaky hand, he discovered one, maybe two broken ribs. He lay back on the bed exhausted.

When he woke up, Justo was sitting beside the bed, smiling. "You know, General," the terrorist said, "many people would think that holding out is not smart. But I admire you. If you were younger—if you were Basque—I might offer you a job. . . ."

"I fought in Basque country once," West grunted.

"Yes," said the terrorist, "and you lost."

"You'll lose, too, you son of a bitch."

"No," Justo said calmly. "We'll win. With Franco dead all these years, anything is now possible."

"Then your new country'll nickel and dime itself to death," said the general, wincing in pain. "You'll just shrivel up and die."

"Therefore foreign aid," Justo said, smiling again.

"Do you know what you're buying into if you take Soviet money?" West said, glaring at the Spaniard.

"I expect they will try to treat us much like Cuba."

"Damn right they would," West nodded, ignoring the pain. "Is that why you fight your war, or whatever you call it? If you love the Soviets so damn much, why don't you move to Moscow?"

"So, you see my problem perfectly," Justo said. "In order to gain the freedom of my people, I have no practical choice but to accept the help of the Soviets. Once I do this—*ola!* My country is no longer free. A real mess, no?"

"Something on your mind, kid?" West asked, "or are you just shooting the breeze with a dead man?"

"General," Justo said, "I have more interest in keeping you alive than in letting Stok kill you. As long as the Russian thinks I am cooperating, his people will remain happy. However, two things concern me."

"The prisoners," West said.

"Yes. I want twelve political prisoners released for your freedom. That is the first thing. Your well-being is the second. Life would look so much more hopeful to me, if I had a powerful and influential friend in Washington. Someone to put forward my case when the time comes."

"You want to play both ends against the middle, don't you, kid? You'll use the Soviets if all else fails, but you'd rather use the U.S.A., right?"

"I believe the Americans would agree to create new industry in a friendly socialist state."

"We're progressive, kid," West replied, "but we're not *that* goddamn progressive."

"Your country might prefer to have us as an ally than let the Soviets get a Mediterranean port."

West looked at the terrorist.

The Spaniard gazed back, eyes bright with enthusiasm. "It is only important that I, a poor peasant's son, will have an influential contact in Washington. You do not have to agree or disagree, General. Let me call you George. You will remain alive, George. But please, I would ask of you to take better care of your health." Justo grinned again.

"Where'd a poor peasant's son learn your kind of English?" West said in his deep voice.

"At Harvard Law School," Justo said. "Now rest. You must be on your guard today. Stok has a new approach."

THE RUSSIAN FUMBLED with a syringe and some vials. "You have the honor, General," he said, "of being our first guinea pig with this drug. Frankly, I hope it kills you. But not before we get our information." Stok was unable to manipulate the needle and anger flashed across his face. "You," he snapped at the BNF guard, "inject him with this."

The general tried to make it as hard on the man as he could. He shifted in his chair, but the bindings prevented even the smallest body movement.

He was alarmed at how good he felt when the serum began coursing through his body. He welcomed it as an exhausted man welcomes a deep, restful sleep.

A woman's alluring voice called him out of his slumber. "George," it said, "George, it's Angela. Please, George, you must tell me everything."

George West began to talk.

BACK IN THE DARK CELL, West cursed himself for a traitor and seven kinds of fool. It should have been obvious that no woman as beautiful and as young as Angela would ever be interested in such a decrepit old fart. Under the influence of some new drug, he'd told a strange woman everything. Worst of all, now that the drug had worn off, he remembered everything about the session.

The KGB bastard had beat him after all. They had everything they wanted.

George West lay in his cell waiting to die.

He must have slept because he did not notice the big man enter the room. A crack of light from the door showed the man's silhouette close to his cot. West could see the outline of a huge pistol in the man's hand. "I'd like it in the heart," he said. His voice was so controlled and distinct that it surprised him. "I'd like it fast and professional. Two shots."

Mack Bolan's spirit sank when he heard West's words. He wondered how the BNF could have so completely broken his friend, a man he had admired for years, since before the Terrorist Wars. "I never thought of you as a quitter, General," he said. There was a pause.

"Executioner!" West sat upright on the cot. He grunted from the pain of the sudden movement.

Bolan smiled in the dark. There was only one man who insisted on calling him by that name. Only one man he allowed to freely use that word to describe him. Whenever George Armstrong West called him Executioner there was an edge of professional respect in the man's voice. Bolan remembered a night's drinking before the Tet Offensive when West had waxed eloquent about The Executioner's calling.

"Never forget that yours is an old, necessary and respected profession," West had said, "and that you are the best of the best. I worry about losing other men—I worry about their missions and I worry about the work turning them into animals. But you, Sergeant, I never worry about you."

Now George West gripped Bolan's free arm. "Listen, Mack, I have work for you. There's a KGB bastard in this building who knows too much. He'll have tapes. We have to get him!"

Bolan flashed a penlight over George's figure and whistled in the dark. "I'm glad your voice sounds like you, General. I wouldn't have recognized your face."

"That bad, eh?"

"Bad enough. How do you feel?"

"I can walk. Maybe."

"Take these, they'll help." Bolan offered him several pink

tablets. "They're Dexedrine. They're sold over the counter here. You'll need the energy."

"I could use a body transplant, Mack," the old man growled. He gulped down the tablets.

"How did you find me?"

"I followed the girl whose voice you heard," Bolan said.

West looked at the black-clad man in astonishment.

"I brought her here," Bolan said. "She's one of the Stony Man people, works with April Rose back at the Farm. You know about my thing there."

"But how the hell did you get inside? Why do Stok and Justo think she's one of them?"

"She let me in. And she *is* one of them. She's been on advance infiltration since your telex to me about terrorist pressure in Spain. She works fast. Nobody's stopped her yet and she gets what she wants. She's good."

"Do you have another gun?" West asked him.

"There's a guard outside the door with a Skorpion and some extra clips," Bolan replied. "He's not in a condition to use them."

THE RUSSIAN WAS EASY TO FIND. He and Justo sent their angry voices tumbling into the hallway. Stok shouted something about needing to control the tapes, and Justo stormed out into the corridor. He marched away from the Americans, unaware of their presence. A short laugh from Stok followed him down the corridor.

"We've got to do this real fast, General," Bolan whispered. "Our diversion is due in minutes."

The pills Bolan had given him were working. He was thinking clearly now for the first time in days. West made the gesture of pulling a pin on a grenade. Bolan nodded.

The nightfighter took two M-26s from his blacksuit. He

sidled up to the door. With one grenade in each hand Bolan held out the pins to West. Then in one quick step The Executioner pivoted and tossed two activated calling cards into the room in an underhand sweep.

West marveled at how Bolan pivoted on the other foot and came to rest on the other side of the doorframe with his AutoMag drawn. The whole movement had been as effortless and natural as that of a cat. A big cat.

Hell broke loose inside the room. The powerful double blast sent debris scattering in a fan pattern from the doorway.

The general was first in. He sprayed everything on the floor with the Skorpion Bolan had given him. Then Bolan entered and opened up likewise, gun and man fused as one. Stok lay in a puddle of gore with half his torso blown away. The man was still moving. West ended it with a mercy spray to the Russian's head.

On the floor by the doorway, Bolan found the three small spools of tape. He scooped them up and stuffed them inside his shirt.

They heard the running footfalls of the BNF guards. A heavy explosion rocked the building, followed by more and louder explosions. Just in time, Bolan thought. The guards reached the doorway and West chopped and diced them with autofire. Three bodies fell in a heap at the entrance.

"Those pills work," West said.

Bolan looked at the old man with a new appreciation. In Nam, they had known of each other's activities by reputation only. This was the first time they had seen each other in action.

FROM THE SIDE DOOR OF THE BUILDING, they could see huge flashes light the night from behind a stand of trees. The Laser Wagon was on automatic kill, timed and primed to pound the compound with a potent hellfire. Bolan and the general spotted BNF troops at irregular intervals between themselves and the wagon. As the barrage continued, the incoming fire fast approaching their position, Bolan motioned to West that they sweep around the BNF flank and make for the artillery's flash. West nodded. Bolan tossed the KGB tapes through the collapsed wall of a burning clapboard toolshed hit by the wagon-fire. Gripping the AutoMag, he backed away from the blaze, satisfied.

In the open now, both men bobbed and weaved, creating long shadows that crisscrossed as they dashed. Bolan was last into the cover of the trees. He tossed a grenade at an BNF cluster who still faced the wagon. The terrorists could not see the vehicle for the trees. They did not see the grenade, either.

IN THE LASER WAGON, Mack started the engine and canceled the pattern of automatic fire. "There's some Armalites in back, General," Bolan said, jerking his thumb. "I've got a feeling we'll have some company down the road." He fed gas to the armored vehicle, popped the gears; they made the road with their headlights off.

In the side mirror, West caught a glimpse of pursuit. "Company's comin'," he said. "Can this thing fire backward?"

Bolan motioned behind him to the inboard computer console, but the general looked at it in disgust. "That'd take me a week to figure out," he said. Bolan nodded and gunned the wagon, but the pursuers were closing. They roared down the winding road.

"Where are we, Mack?"

"Near Roncesvaux," Bolan replied, making a tight turn with the hurtling machine. "France is coming up in about thirty minutes but I guess we can't hold 'em that long."

"Roadblock," West said as they rounded the corner. "Cut it to the right."

The bulk of the vehicle tipped onto two wheels but remained upright. Bolan gripped the steering wheel tight as the wide-bodied van held to the punishing swerve. He accelerated and the wagon fishtailed off into brush, bouncing over small boulders, crashing through the brittle vegetation that filled a gully running behind the long sandy hill between them and the roadblock.

The pursuit vehicle overshot the Laser Wagon's sudden turnoff and came to a stop at the roadblock.

"Okay, we bought a little time," growled the general. "Now the hell what?"

BACK AT THE ROADBLOCK Justo was enraged. Yes, he had wanted the general to live. Yes, he had wanted the KGB agent to die. But he also wanted the prisoners. His own brother was among them and when Bolan crashed into the undergrowth, Justo lost a hold on the one last chance of his brother's freedom. "Turn it around!" he shouted to all in hearing range. "Get that wagon and bring it back here. Get after it!"

MACK BOLAN WINCED as the gully came to an abrupt end in rocks and wild oak. The way was impassable. The idea of backing up the route they had come appealed to Bolan like water appealed to cats. "Let me at that console," he said, pushing past the general's seat.

The minute the BNF cars came into view the Laser Wagon opened up with a fire of slugs and shells that ripped the air. Tongues of flame flashed in the night. The multifire licked its way into the approaching cars. The lead car was split in two. A survivor spilled out and scrambled for cover.

The second car smashed to a stop in the gravel and disgorged two forms that dashed behind a rocky outcrop, one of them waving to the backup vehicles. The other man was aiming an RPG-7 at the wagon. "No, Jimenez!" Justo yelled. "We need them alive."

The leader signaled the squads in the other cars to get out and form into two groups. Together the squads would approach the wagon in a pincer movement. They moved out, just as the second car received a direct hit from the Laser Wagon's sensor-organized shelling.

The pattern of fire changed sluggishly but soon it was damaging the cover of rocks and trees into which the BNF had moved. It continued to harry the men as they clambered toward the wagon. The man with the rocket launcher was tossed aside by an incoming blast. The man next to him was opened at the abdomen like a ripe melon cracked on a rock.

Jimenez recovered his footing. In fury at his pain, he struggled to raise the RPG to his bleeding shoulder. He aimed it at the Laser Wagon, fired it with reckless impatience.

The desperate blast hit home. A five-pound grenade made contact with the wagon at a range of less than three hundred yards. The explosive had the capacity of piercing armor plate to a depth of 12.6 inches. It demolished the passenger side of the front cab, an area especially vulnerable because the window was strangely left open.

Smoke began to belch from the interior. The hole blown by the grenade spewed out crackling flames.

The Laser Wagon burned. The terrorist wars claimed a war wagon as surely as had the Mafia war.

"You idiot," Justo screamed. He scrambled up the hill toward Jimenez. "You fucking idiot." As he ran he pulled the ancient Tokarev from his belt and fired at his own man. The second slug caught Jimenez in the head. Justo kicked the rocket launcher away from the dead man's hands.

He shouted to the survivors. "Get up there and get them out. If they're still alive, don't kill them!"

Both arms of the attack left their cover and moved toward the smoking Laser Wagon. The pointman reached the hole in its front end and turned back with a puzzled expression. "There's no one inside," he said.

Two of the quickest men whirled and began firing int opposite flanks but they were too late. On either flank, Bola and the general opened fire with the Armalites.

Death in the form of 5.56mm slugs rained down on the BNF unit.

The general broke cover to shoot toward a better angle. A 7.62mm steel core from a Kalashnikov smacked through hi belly. West was on his knees now, but he was still firing. The unit went down almost to a man.

Bolan whirled in position and aimed his AR-18 down the hil toward Justo. "Out in the open," he shouted at the onl survivor.

Justo walked from the smoke with his hands raised. He looked up at the two men, climbed the hill and came to stand near the general. "I told you to take better care of your health George," he said.

"You've lost your friend in Washington," West answered him. "I'm hit bad."

Bolan approached them with the Armalite trained on Justo "Is it the belly?" he asked. West nodded. "We've got no transport," Bolan said apologetically. West nodded again.

"Help me carry him to that tree," Bolan told Justo. Together they made a fireman's chair and carried the fallen man to the spot Bolan indicated.

"Where's the girl?" Bolan asked the BNF man.

"I let her go. She asked to leave the safehouse and I let her. I was before your attack."

"You did something right."

"I let you kill Stok. That's what I did right." Justo turned to West. "General," he said, "I am genuinely sorry that you are going to die."

"How the hell do you think *I* feel," the general joked. His grin turned to a wince of pain. "Mack," he said, "what do you think? You think Justo here is a reasonable man?"

"Maybe so. You tell me."

"Ah, Executioner," West exclaimed, "all I gotta say is thanks. Executioner, you've helped this stupid old man turn the whole thing around. I was down, Mack. I was way down, I'd given in back there. All that was left was to nail up the box. But hell, Executioner!" West boomed against his death. "You helped me bounce back. You helped me come back and win. Everything I lost I got back with your help, you hear me? I wouldn't trade today's action for another decade of pushing paper and meeting old men. It's a good day to die, Executioner."

JUSTO SAT BESIDE THE GENERAL till the end. Occasionally he held a cigarette to the man's mouth and talked a little bit about how he saw the future of his country.

Toward morning when the general died, Justo closed the old soldier's eyes and spoke to Mack. "American, you liked this man, no?"

Bolan nodded.

"I want to bury him here, American. Okay? I would like to bring my brother's sons here and tell them the story of this fine general. It's a good place, no?"

Bolan nodded. The man tore a strip of rocker panel from the devastated Laser Wagon. He began to scrape at the earth under the general's tree.

Mack Bolan picked up his weapon and headed down the pass toward France. The general's words echoed in his mind as he walked.

Bounce back, George had said. It had worked for him, and it worked for Bolan. Bounce back was the name of the maneuver they'd used to sucker the BNF into the firing zone around the Laser Wagon.

In the last combat strategy of his life, the general had found a way to bounce back himself.

For Bolan, the maneuver had cost a dear friend and an unusual vehicle.

He turned to look back up the parched hillside. Etched against the earth he saw the figure of Justo, bent over, digging with the makeshift shovel. In the searing sunlight the charred form of the Laser Wagon stood like a sentinel behind him, a hollow shell on ash-flecked flattened tires.

"To hell with the vehicle," he muttered, "but the man I'll sorely miss."

He turned and trotted down the stony hillside, leaving Justo to figure out his own fate.

There would be more blood spilled by soldiers of the right side in these terrorist wars, maybe more than Bolan cared to think about, maybe blood close to home. But for now he knew only that one man's departure on the battlefield heralded a new departure for himself. No more Laser Wagon for support meant a return to total reliance on his own honed skills.

And that was fine with Bolan.

West dead. Harrison in Washington dead. Eve Aguilar dead. The toll climbed. He had that feeling again that he'd be on his own in the days to come, back to himself again. For the paths of fire beckoned to him alone.

He left the burial ground, cemetery not only for a gut-shot soldier and bombed-out war wagon but a terrorist's will as well, and walked into the heat.

THE COMBAT CATALOG

Armbrust Disposable Anti-Tank Weapon

The Armbrust (crossbow) is a shoulder-fired antitank weapon that produces no smoke, flash or blast. Can be fired from small enclosed spaces by one man, with no more than a pistol-shot sound. Countermass of plastic flakes eliminates recoil; firing pistons brake at each end of the tube to seal in flash and gases. The Armbrust is supplied as separate sealed rounds, which are disposed of after firing. One man can comfortably carry four rounds.

With a maximum range of 1,500 meters, and capable of penetrating an armored vehicle at 300 meters, the Armbrust is a highly dangerous, highly portable weapon. Also fires an anti-personnel fragmentation round that cuts down whole groups of enemies in a single gore-blast. Sometimes called Armburst by fans.

Length: 850mm
Maximum tube diameter: 78mm
Muzzle velocity: 220 m/s
Weight: 6.3kilogram weapon, .99kilogram warhead
Warhead caliber: 67mm
Flight time to 300 meters: 1.5 seconds
Maximum obliquity for armor penetration: 78 degrees

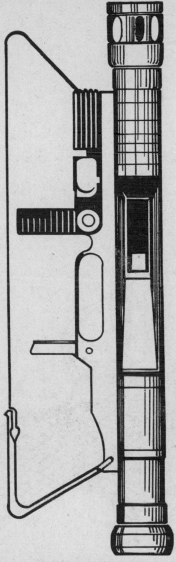

Armbrust Disposable Anti-Tank Weapon

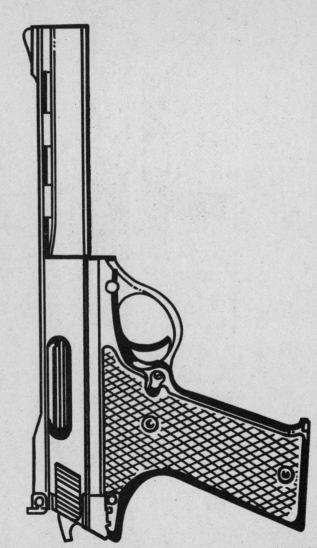

.44 AutoMag

.44 AutoMag

"The Flesh Shredder." Automatic handgun of impressive size, weight and recoil. Gun designed around a wildcat cartridge, the .44 Auto Magnum, produced by marrying a .44 revolver bullet with a cut-down 7.62mm NATO rifle cartridge case.

A recoil-operated pistol with a rotating bolt head controlled by cam tracks in the pistol frame, the series C AutoMag fires a 240-grain bullet at a muzzle velocity of 1,640 feet per second with muzzle energy of 1,455 lbs. Requires a bolt with six locking lugs to contain explosive internal gas pressures.

Its 6.5-inch barrel makes the AutoMag 11.5 inches in length. Unloaded, it weighs almost four pounds. A silver monster, the AutoMag is as close to a rifle as any handgun can be. Massive recoil demands powerful grasp. Its 240-grain boattail slug can tear through the solid metal of an automobile engine block.

Atchisson Automatic Shotgun

An automatic 12-bore shotgun styled like an assault rifle. This butcher fires 12-gauge shells in semiauto, three-shot burst or full-auto slaughter. The Atchisson looks much like the M-16 rifle but is larger and heavier, with a 14-inch barrel. Takes a 7-round box magazine or with modification a 20-round box mag of shells packed with a mix of 50 number-two and double-ought steel balls. Heavy, short-range firepower showers steel balls at 366 meters per second. The Atchisson takes no prisoners.

Absolutely
no illustrations
available
of the Atchisson

M-1911 Colt .45 Government Model

The Government Model is an automatic pistol based on a design patented by John M. Browning in 1897. One of the most successful pistols of the twentieth century, widely copied and produced under license in many countries of the world. The Government Model has been standard issue to U.S. officers since 1911. An improved version M-1911 A-1 dating from 1926 is the sturdiest weapon in its class. A heavy, bulky and reliable gun, the Government Model is the man-stopper of our times.

The Government Model has been modified for Bolan's men with:

- Parkerized black finish
- semiauto or three-shot death bursts
- blunt suppressor
- modified and shortened slide
- fold-down lever and enlarged trigger guard for two-hand hold
- increased twist of barrel rifling to increase accuracy and cut bullet velocity
- phosphorous sights
- 7-, 10- and 15-round magazine

C-4 Plastic Explosive Compound

Composition 4 is a military plastic explosive consisting of 90% RDX (Hexogen) and 10% polyisobutylene plasticizer. This destruction putty is a harmless-looking malleable plastic compound, easily molded onto target.

Hexogen is the foremost high brisance explosive, owing to its high density and high detonation velocity. Relatively insensitive and very stable; performance properties only slightly inferior to HMX (Octogen).

Heat of Explosion: 1439 kcal/kg

Melting point: 204°C

Impact sensitivity: 0.75 kp m

Detonation velocity: 8,750 meters per second

Weatherby Mark V Rifle

Bolt-action .460 Magnum hunting rifle. Developed by Roy Weatherby, whose theories on ballistics (involving light, high-velocity bullets) revolutionized big-game hunting. Five-hundred-grain bullet achieves highest velocity of any bullet in the world. A monster in both power and size, with a 26-inch chrome-lined barrel and overall length of 46.5 inches, the Mark V is short of four feet long and weighs 10.5 lbs. Bolt sleeve enclosed from the rear; incredibly strong action made entirely from steel, no alloy parts. Streamlined action weighs only 36 oz. Shotgun-type buttplate with ventilated rubber recoil pad to handle the 100 lbs. of free recoil.

Nondetachable staggered box magazine holds two shots. Achieves muzzle velocity of 2,700 feet per second, 2,300 fps at 100 yards, 2,005 fps at 200 yards, 1,730 fps at 300 yards. Energy at muzzle is a thundering 8,095 foot-pounds, 6,025 at 100 yards, 4,465 at 200 yards, 3,320 at 300 yards. Midrange trajectory at 100 yards: +0.7 inches.

High-powered hunting rifle with massive stopping power, wielded by the strongest shootists only.

Beretta 93-R

An advanced self-loading pistol, the 93-R can fire either single shots or three-round bursts. For distant or difficult shots, a small front handgrip folds down for the left hand; left thumb hooks through extended trigger guard for extra control. Folding carbine stock can be clipped onto butt for shoulder firing, transforming an apparently ordinary self-loading pistol into a deadly accurate machine pistol.

Fires 9mm parabellum rounds; short recoil operation, hinged block locking. Detachable box magazine, 15 or 20 rounds. Achieves muzzle velocity of 375 meters per second. With 15-round box and carbine metal stock, the 93-R weighs 1.39 kg. Length of gun minus stock, 240mm. Rate of fire: 110 rounds per minute.

Modified for Mack Bolan with suppressor and specially machined springs designed to cycle subsonic cartridges, effectively silencing the weapon. Flashhider for night firing. The 93-R eliminates opponents precisely, silently and invisibly.

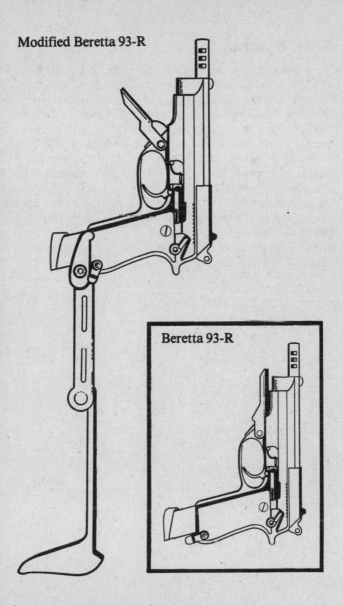

Modified Beretta 93-R

Beretta 93-R

Colt Commando

The Commando is a chopped version of the Colt manufactured M16A1 that was developed for the U.S. Special Forces in Vietnam. The ten-inch (254mm) barrel of the submachine gun, instead of the twenty-one inch barrel (508mm) of the assault rifle, produces a very large muzzle-flash, which makes it necessary to incorporate a four-inch flash hider that can be unscrewed when necessary. The weapon features selective fire and a holding-open device, and is actuated by the same direct gas action as the M16A1. The Commando also has a telescopic butt. In addition to its close-quarters battle use by the Special Forces, it is also believed to be in limited use by the British Special Air Service.

Weight: 2.97 kg. Length: 711mm

Rifling: 4 grooves RH Muzzle velocity: 915 m/s

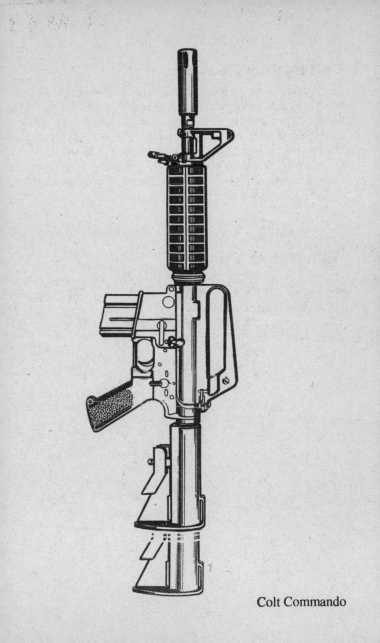

Colt Commando

Colt Python Revolver

The Python is built upon the .41 caliber big brother of the
Model D frame. This .357 Magnum is one of the leading police
handguns in the U.S. Solid frame design; swing-out cylinder;
double-single action. Though revolvers have a slower rate of
fire and take longer to load than automatic pistols, the Python's
gore-making power is the source of its fame. Used by Able
Team with magnaported 152mm barrel, 158-grain hollowpoint
slug and speedloader.

Colt Cobra Model D3

The Cobra is a caliber .38 Special six-shot pistol. It is 222mm
long with a 101mm barrel, yet weighs only .42 kilograms.
Though not quite as powerful as other pistols in the arsenal, the
Cobra hurls a 200-grain slug with a muzzle velocity of 223
meters per second.

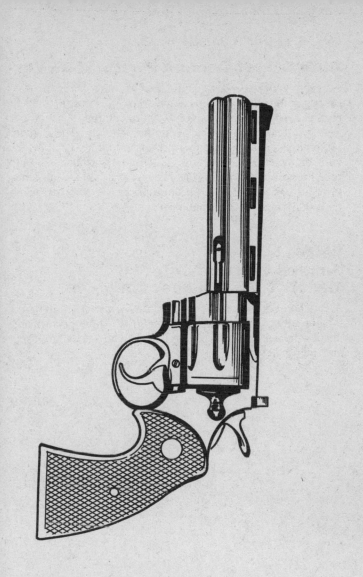

Colt Python

Detonics .45 Combat Master Mark VI

A recently developed weapon, the Detonics .45 is a heavy caliber automatic pistol of compact size. Comes throated for high-performance ammunition with an enlarged ejection port to ensure that empty cartridges do not hang up. The Detonics .45 obtains excellent stopping power from a heavy bullet and large diameter, yet it is not substantially larger than a .38 snub-nosed revolver. A stainless-steel beauty that, fitted with rubber grips, is easily controlled, despite the massive recoil. A big-bore skull-smasher in a small package.

Smith & Wesson
Model 19 .357 Combat Magnum

A six-shot .357 Magnum, 242mm long with a 101mm barrel. Weight: .89kg. The Combat Magnum is a high-performance pistol with skull-popping power. Comes with a fixed front sight and micrometer rear sight.

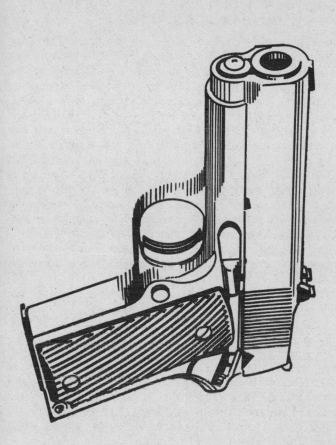

Detonics .45 Combat Master Mark VI

Heckler & Koch
G-11 Caseless Assault Rifle

The G-11 is undoubtedly a unique gun that promises to set a new standard in the small-arms world. NATO had investigated the idea of caseless guns in the mid-sixties, but dropped the idea shortly after 1967. The West German government, meanwhile, was pursuing the idea of an improved infantry weapon with a better chance of a hit than any gun in existence. The proposed gun was also to fulfill the FINABEL range and rate of fire characteristics. H&K met the challenge with a radically new design that was the caseless G-11.

The G-11's smooth outer casing, with virtually no protuberances or holes, sets it apart from all other guns. There are only two holes: the muzzle and the ejection opening for clearing misfired rounds. The plastic casing provides complete protection for the mechanism against shocks, rough handling, immersion, frost, dust and dirt. The pistol grip is at the point of balance; the optical sight is in the carrying handle above the receiver.

The round is a bullet set into a solid block of propellant: with no empty case to be cleared and ejected, the time and movement of the firing cycle is reduced considerably. The result is greatly increased cycle speed, and in fact the G-11 can fire so rapidly—2,000 rounds per minute—that the third round of a 3-round burst has already left the gun before the recoil has begun. On autofiring the G-11 uses "floating firing" to smooth out recoil; rate of fire is 600 rounds per minute and recoil is light and smooth. Three-round bursts are fired within 90 milliseconds. Though the G-11 round is only 4.7mm caliber, it can penetrate a steel helmet from more than 500 meters.

The G-11 in the hands of Mack Bolan's chosen few is more than just a gun—it is the ultimate death tool of the Executioner.

Dimensions: 750mm long, 65mm wide and 298mm high
Length of Barrel: 540mm
Weight with 100 rounds: 4.5kg
Cooling: air
Rifling profile: polygonal

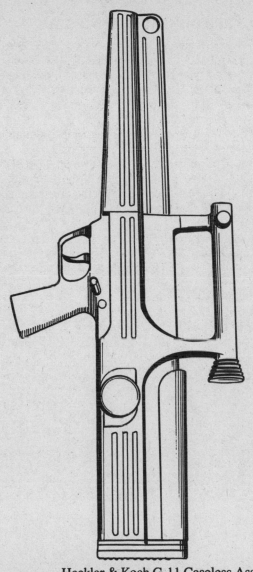

Heckler & Koch G-11 Caseless Assault Rifle

Heckler & Koch MP-5 SD-3 SMG

The MP-5 series of submachine guns was developed from the highly successful G-3 rifle and adopted in 1966 by the police forces and border guards of West Germany. Fires single-shot, full automatic or in 3-, 4- or 5-round bursts. The MP-5 is unusual for an SMG in that it fires from a closed breech position using a hammer notch.

The MP-5 SD-3 is a silenced version, using a 40mm modular pure muffler-type silencer. Reduces muzzle velocity of bullet to subsonic level, eliminating the shock wave. The SD-3 also features a retractable buttstock, which shortens the overall length of the gun. More accurate than the conventional SMG because of closed-bolt firing, the SD-3 is a compact, accurate kill machine.

Operation: Delayed blowback
Feed: 15- or 30-round curved box magazine
Weight: 3.4 kilograms Weight with 30-round magazine: 3.92 kilograms
Cartridge: 9mm parabellum
Muzzle velocity: 285 m/s
Cyclic rate of fire: 800 rounds per minute

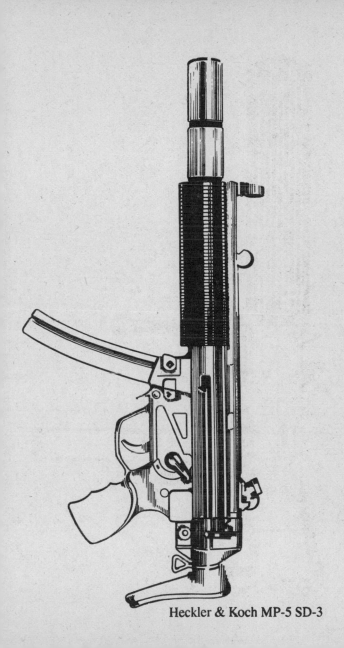

Heckler & Koch MP-5 SD-3

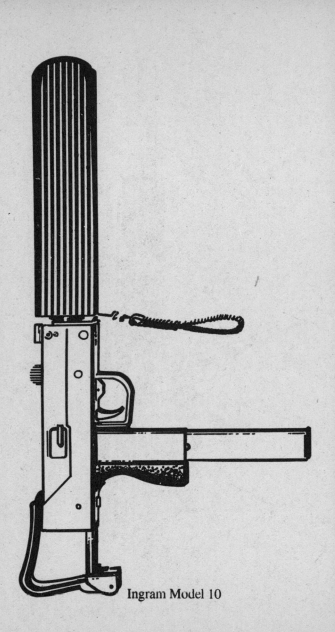

Ingram Model 10

Ingram Model 10 Submachine Gun

Very short, very compact SMG. Bolan's latest model is chambered for .45 ACP rounds in 30-round magazine. Uses stamped metal components, an overhung bolt of sheet steel weighted with lead, and barrel threaded to take suppressor. Easily concealed.

Weight when empty: 2.84 kg; loaded with 30 rounds .45 ACP, 3.82 kg. Length with telescoped stock 269mm. Barrel length 146mm. Suppressor weighs .545 kg, and is 291mm long. Barrel rifling: 6 grooves RH; for .45 ACP rounds, 1 turn in 508mm. Muzzle velocity: 280 meters per second with .45 ACP, at a cyclic rate of 1,145 rounds per minute.

Bolan uses MAC suppressor. The MAC reduces emergent gas velocity to subsonic level. Target hears only the crack that the bullet carries with it. Suppressor tube covered with Nomex-A heat-resistant material. Also comes with long barrel for increased range and improved bullet power.

Wraparound bolt keeps the center of gravity over the pistol grip for steady one-handed firing. Compact, close-range weapon can deliver decimating firepower in quiet but potent bursts.

MM-1 Multiround Projectile Launcher

A squat, fearsome-looking weapon, the MM-1 is a spring-powered projectile launcher that can fire any combination of smoke, tear gas, flare or explosive rounds. The MM-1 is loaded as is a revolver, the operator choosing any order and combination of projectiles. With an effective range of 120 meters, the MM-1 is a one-man terrorist controller. The launcher can hurl twelve rounds of confusion and destruction in as little as five seconds with no appreciable recoil.

Caliber: 38mm
Weight, loaded: 9 kilograms
Length: 546mm

LAW 80 Rocket Launcher

A recently developed state-of-the-art rocket launcher under trial by the British army. Detailed performance figures are still classified. The LAW 80 is a one-shot disposable weapon with a range and lethality superior to the M-72. The weapon is designed to incapacitate all armored vehicles found on the battlefield through the 1980s and beyond, from all angles of attack including frontal. The LAW 80 is larger and heavier than others of its function owing to the emphasis on increased accuracy. The launcher incorporates a spotting rifle to test aim; barrel and mechanism of rifle are contained in a bulge below the disposable tube. The x1 reflex collinator sight folds over outer tube.

The LAW 80's HEAT round is rocket propelled, using a short-burning rocket that burns in the tube, leaving the missile to coast to target and wreak its pulverizing effects.

Length: 1,000mm folded, 1,500mm extended
Construction: grp
Warhead: 94mm hollow charge
Effective range: 500 meters

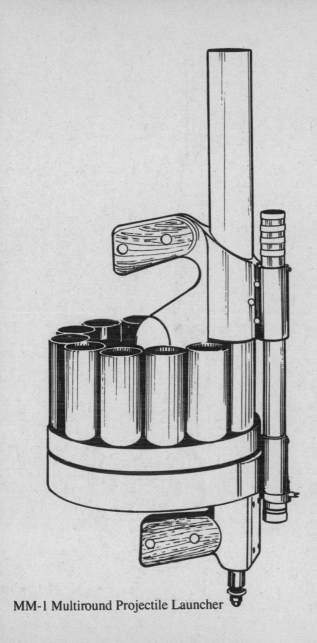

MM-1 Multiround Projectile Launcher

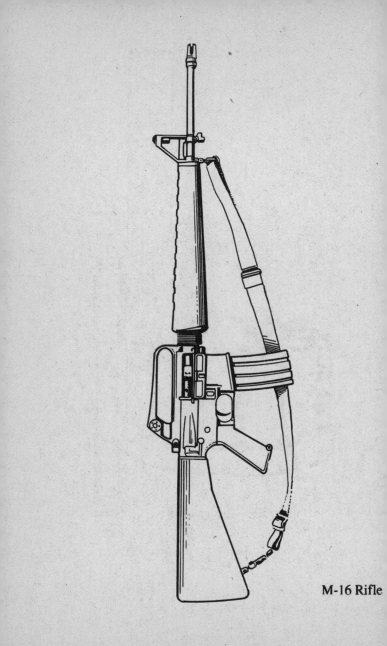

M-16 Rifle

M-16 Rifle

This Vietnam veteran fires a 5.56mm caliber cartridge at high velocity, can puncture an army helmet at 500 meters. A lightweight, low-impulse rifle, the M-16 weighs 3.1 kgs. Gas direct-fire operation using a rotating bolt lock. Uses 20- or 30-round magazine.

Rounds use tubular IMR propellant. Buffer modified to control rate of fire. Chamber is chromium-plated.

M-16 with sling and loaded 30-round magazine weighs only 3.73 kg. Trigger pull: 2.3-3.8kp. Length with flash suppressor 990mm, barrel 508mm. Barrel rifling: 6 grooves RH, one turn in 305mm. Muzzle velocity 1000 meters per second. Cyclic firing rate between 700 and 950 rounds per minute. Effective range: 400 meters.

A lightweight supermodern automatic rifle, the M-16's controversial handling qualities make it a deadly weapon for a wide range of clandestine operations.

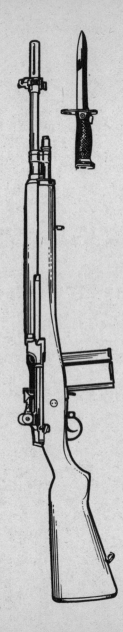

M-14 Rifle

M-14 Rifle

Adopted in 1957 as the standard rifle of the U.S. Army, the M-14 is the ultimate development of the M-1. While retaining the simplicity and reliability of the M-1, the M-14 incorporates an improved magazine that allows full magazines to be loaded onto the rifle without using the unsatisfactory clip of the M-1. The gas port was moved back from the muzzle to about two-thirds of the way up the barrel to prevent any interference with accuracy and consistency of firing. The M-1's operating rod and cam were modified for the M-14 for a more gentle push on the piston. The result was steadier firing, with the sights brought back to target faster. The M-14 was the first weapon in the U.S. Army to fire the NATO round. A high-quality, accurate weapon with indispensable bayonet for beyond the front lines.

Length with flash suppressor: 1,120mm
Barrel length: 559mm
Weight with full magazine and cleaning kit: 5.1 kg
Muzzle velocity: 853 m/s
Rate of fire: Cyclic: 700-750 rounds/min

M-203 Grenade Launcher

Developed under the direction of United States Army Weapons
Command, the lightweight M-203 is a single-shot, breech-
loaded, pump action grenade launcher fired from the shoulder
Bolan's is more often than not attached to the underside of the
M-16.

Length 394mm, weight loaded 1.63 kg, combined weight
with the M-16 is 5 kg. A 40mm grenade round achieves muzzle
velocity of 71 meters per second. Range: 400 meters. Effective
range for area targets 350 meters; point target 150 meters.

Ammo types: high explosive, air burst, smokeless and flashless. High-explosive round contains a grenade 38mm in diameter with 35g of explosive. Formed of rectangular-wrapped steel
wire, notched to allow fragmentation.

The M-203 transforms the M-16 automatic rifle into a highly
mobile single-piece destruction unit.

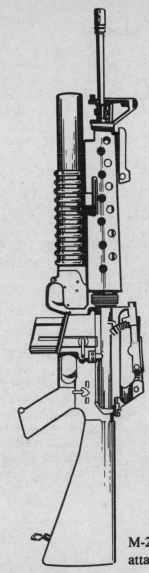

M-203 Grenade Launcher
attached to M-16

M-79 Grenade Launcher

For fifteen years the M-79 has been a highly successful U.S. Army weapon, specifically designed to fire spin-stabilized grenades. A single-shot break-open action breech-loading weapon; highly maneuverable at only 2.95kg loaded. In the hands of one of Bolan's men the M-79 can put 40mm grenades through house windows at a distance of 150 meters. One man with an M-79 and belt full of grenades is a roving destruction unit of frightening accuracy.

Length: 737mm
Barrel length: 356mm
Weight, loaded: 2.95kg
Chamber pressure: 210kg/cm2
Muzzle velocity: 76 m/s
Maximum effective range: 350 meters (area)
150 meters (point)

Mark 19 MOD-3 Automatic Grenade Launcher

The MOD-3 is an air-cooled, blowback-operated automatic machine launcher developed at the Naval Ordnance Depot, Louisville, Kentucky, for use by the U.S. Marines. The MOD-3 destroys armored targets, emplacements, bunkers and helicopters as it hurls 40mm grenades at the incredible rate of 350 to 400 rounds per minute. The MOD-3 can be mounted on vehicles, helicopters or emplacements and fires from a 20-, 50- or 400-round box magazine. Can defeat the frontal protection of an Armored Personnel Carrier from 2,200 meters. Manual or electric firing.

Weight: 35kg
Length: 1,028mm
Height: 206mm
Muzzle velocity: 240 m/s

Misar MU 50-G Hand Grenade

A controlled-effect munition, the MU 50 series has a variety of fragment sizes for specialized killing. Fitted with a silent, flashless and smokeless igniter and delay, which leave no trace behind them when thrown. The MU 50 series grenades are small and light, almost spherical in shape, and can be thrown with greater precision and to a greater range than traditional grenades. The MU 50 also can be fired from the Franchi SPAS 12 special-purpose shotgun.

Made with a plastic shell containing a matrix of fragments, the MU 50-G hurls steel beads at 6,100 meters per second, with a kill radius of five meters. The MU 50-G means instant carnage.

Length: 70mm
Diameter: 46mm
Safety range: 20m
Weight: grenade: 140 grams
       explosive: 50 grams

Stoner 63 System

The Stoner 63 is the brainchild of Eugene Stoner, designer at Armalite and creator of the AR-15 (M-16). The Stoner 63 is actually a six-weapon system that uses interchangeable parts to permit on-the-spot transformation into an assault rifle, submachine gun, medium machine gun, fixed (tank) machine gun and two light machine guns (magazine-fed and belt-fed).

Unlike the AR-10 and AR-15, each of which uses a gas system, the Stoner 63 uses a conventional long-stroke piston. The rifle and SMG are both hammer-fired from a closed-bolt position and have selective fire; the machine guns fire 5.56mm rounds from the open-bolt position and have fixed firing pins controlled by the piston extension; the receiver is inverted.

The Stoner is a tactical weapon with demoralizing versatility; turns one man into an arsenal of firepower.

Uzi Submachine Gun

Developed by the Israeli army in the early fifties, the Uzi is modeled mainly on the Czech Models 23 and 25 submachine guns. This blowback weapon has an overhung bolt, reducing the length of the gun to 470mm with its metal butt folded, and only 640mm with butt extended for accurate firing from the shoulder. A 32-round magazine enters the pistol grip, increasing magazine rigidity and making reloading in darkness easier. To increase firepower, two magazines are welded together at right angles: when both are full, one extends forward under and parallel to the barrel; when one is empty, it extends backward. Added magazine increases weight at the front of the gun to prevent muzzle climb during auto firing.

Body is strengthened by the formation of fullering grooves which make it easier to handle in adverse operating conditions. Intelligent use of sheet-metal stampings and plastics results in weight of 3.5 kg. Barrel rifling: 4 grooves RH, 1 turn in 245mm. Firing 600 9mm parabellum rounds per minute, the gun is capable of unleashing a full magazine in just over three seconds, at a muzzle velocity of 420 meters per second. Effective range: 200 meters. Mack Bolan's Uzi is modified with flash-hider for undetected night firing.

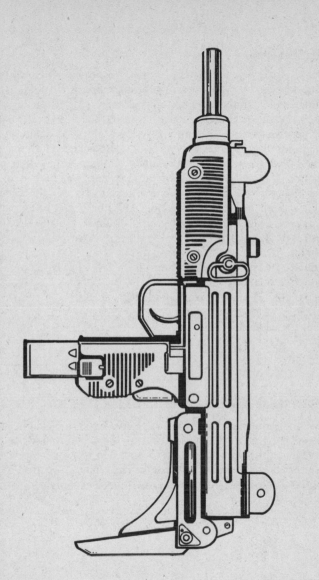

Uzi Submachine Gun

Mini-Uzi

The mini-Uzi resembles its highly respected parent in all aspects of its operation. This blowback-operated submachine gun with the wraparound bolt provides the same efficiency and accuracy of the larger Uzi but in a considerably smaller and lighter weapon. The mini-Uzi is ideal for commando-type operation: it can be easily concealed under normal clothing and yet delivers a lethal 1,200 rounds of 9mm parabellum per minute. Can be fired semi- or full-auto from the hip, or from the shoulder with extended stock. The mini-Uzi is only 360mm in length but still finds room for a 197mm barrel to maintain accuracy. Light, maneuverable, easily hidden, the mini-Uzi is a fistful of 9mm terror.

Length, stock folded: 360mm
Length, stock extended: 600mm
Weight, complete: 2.65 kg
Feed: 20-, 25- and 32-round box magazines
Rifling: 4 grooves RH
Muzzle velocity: 350 m/s
Effective range: 150 meters

Smith & Wesson Model 59 Pistol

A 9mm parabellum self-loading pistol. Though its caliber has been criticized as being insufficiently powerful, the Model 59 carries a 14-round magazine to make up in numbers what it lacks in bore. A death-dealer in the right hands. Weighs .76 kg without magazine; comes with micrometer rear sight.

HE'S EXPLOSIVE.
HE'S MACK BOLAN...
AGAINST ALL ODDS

He learned his deadly skills in Vietnam...then put them to good use by destroying the Mafia in a blazing one-man war. Now **Mack Bolan** is back to battle new threats to freedom—and he's recruited some high-powered forces to help...**Able Team**—Bolan's famous Death Squad from the Mafia wars—now reborn to tackle urban savagery too vicious for regular law enforcement. And **Phoenix Force**—five extraordinary warriors handpicked by Bolan to fight the dirtiest of anti-terrorist wars around the world.

Fight alongside these three courageous forces for freedom in all-new, pulse-pounding action-adventure novels! Travel to the jungles of South America, the scorching sands of the Sahara desert, and the desolate mountains of Turkey. And feel the pressure and excitement building page after page, with non-stop action that keeps you enthralled until the explosive conclusion! Yes, Mack Bolan and his combat teams are living large...and they'll fight against all odds to protect our way of life!

Now you can have all the new Executioner novels delivered right to your home!

You won't want to miss a single one of these exciting new action-adventures. And you don't have to! Just fill out and mail the card at right, and we'll enter your name in the Executioner home subscription plan. You'll then receive four brand-new action-packed books in the Executioner series every other month, delivered right to your home! You'll get two **Mack Bolan** novels, one **Able Team** book and one **Phoenix Force.** No need to worry about sellouts at the bookstore...you'll receive the latest books by mail as soon as they come off the presses. That's four enthralling action novels every other month, featuring all three of the exciting series included in the Executioner library. Mail the card today to start your adventure.

FREE! Mack Bolan bumper sticker.

When we receive your card we'll send your four explosive Executioner novels and, absolutely FREE, a Mack Bolan "Live Large" bumper sticker! This large, colorful bumper sticker will look great on your car, your bulletin board, or anywhere else you want people to know that you like to "live large." And you are under no obligation to buy anything—because your first four books come on a 10-day free trial! If you're not thrilled with these four exciting books, just return them to us and you'll owe nothing. The bumper sticker is yours to keep, FREE!

Don't miss a single one of these thrilling novels...mail the card now, while you're thinking about it. And get the Mack Bolan bumper sticker FREE as our gift!

HE'S UNSTOPPABLE.
AND HE'LL FIGHT
TO DEFEND FREEDOM!

FREE! MACK BOLAN BUMPER STICKER
when you join our home subscription plan.

Gold Eagle Reader Service, a Division of Worldwide Library
2504 W. Southern Avenue, Tempe AZ 85282

YES, please send me my first four Executioner novels, and include my FREE Mack Bolan bumper sticker as a gift. These first four books are mine to examine free for 10 days. If I am not entirely satisfied with these books, I will return them within 10 days and owe nothing. If I decide to keep these novels, I will pay just $1.95 per book (total $7.80). I will then receive the four new Executioner novels every other month as soon as they come off the presses, and will be billed the same low price of $7.80 per shipment. I understand that each shipment will contain two Mack Bolan novels, one Able Team and one Phoenix Force. There are no shipping and handling or any other hidden charges. I may cancel this arrangement at any time, and the bumper sticker is mine to keep as a FREE gift, even if I do not buy any additional books.

166 CIM PACV

Name	(please print)	
Address		Apt No.
City	State	Zip
Signature	(If under 18, parent or guardian must sign.)	

This offer limited to one order per household. We reserve the right to exercise discretion in granting membership. If price changes are necessary, you will be notified. Offer expires August 31, 1984

PRINTED IN U.S.A.

Startron Mark 424 Series 4 Night Vision System

A second-generation night-vision system developed by Smith & Wesson, the Series 4 is a weapon sight meeting military specifications, which mounts directly over the rifle bore. The Series 4 uses a 25mm intensifier tube format to provide a wide field of view; has a microchannel plate amplifier that limits amplification of bright areas for even illumination; and can be fitted with higher power objective lenses, binocular eyepieces and photographic relay lenses. The Series 4 is an advanced night-vision system for use as a viewer in soft probes, and a sniper sight in hard probes.

Length: 292mm
Diameter: 101mm
Weight: 1.7kg
Field of view: 14.5 degrees
Objective focal length: 95mm
Focus range: 25mm to infinity

Walther PPK Pistol

A proved weapon, the PPK was used extensively by the German army in World War II. The PPK was designed for use by police as a concealed weapon (hence the designation "Police Pistol Kriminal") and is actually a smaller version of the 1929 PP. The PPK is a blowback-operated weapon with external hammers and double-action trigger. Fires a 7.65mm (.32 ACP) cartridge from a 7-round detachable box magazine. PPK design copied in Hungary, Turkey and the USSR.

Length: 155mm
Barrel length: 86mm
Weight: 568g
Rifling: 6 grooves RH
Muzzle energy: 186 J
Muzzle velocity: 280 m/s

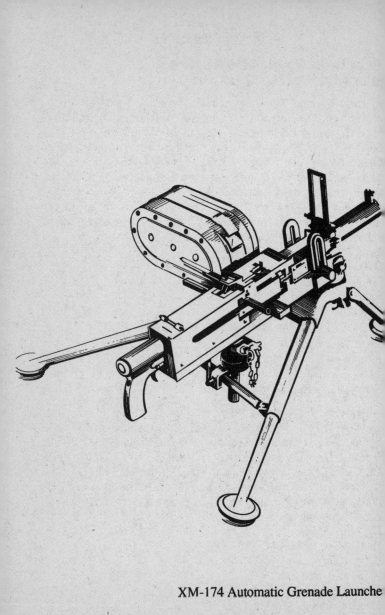

XM-174 Automatic Grenade Launche

XM-174 Automatic Grenade Launcher

The XM-174 is a compact, direct blowback action self-powered launcher that fires standard U.S. Army 40mm low-velocity grenade cartridges from a 12-round magazine.

The XM-174 delivers accurate fire to a range of 400 meters with standard rounds, or up to 1,000 meters with RAP—Rocket Assisted Projectile—rounds. This brutal weapon has a wide variety of combat-tested applications. Fires from bipod, tripod or pindle mounts; used on helicopters, armored vehicles and river-patrol boats. For high maneuverability the XM-174 can be fired from the hip with less recoil than the M-79. Empties a 12-round magazine in just over six seconds of terror. Function: Automatic or semiautomatic.

Length overall: 712mm
Width with magazine: 387mm
Height with magazine: 216mm
Weight of launcher: 7.25kg
Weight of loaded magazine: 4.5kg

ADVISORY
STONY MAN FARM:
Geographical Reference

Shenandoah National Park, Virginia, runs along the crest of the Blue Ridge Mountains from Front Royal (north) to Waynesboro (south), providing spectacular vistas overlooking historic Shenandoah Valley and the Piedmont, said to afford the widest views in the eastern states.

Stony Man Mountain is one of the highest peaks of the region (4010 feet), situated along Skyline Drive about five miles south of the US211 intersection—roughly 80 air miles from Washington. The entire area is heavily forested—hardwoods and conifers—except for an occasional grassy meadow along the crest.

Skyline Drive is the only throughway running north-south along the crest. At Waynesboro, it links up with the Blue Ridge Parkway which runs for 471 miles to Great Smokies National Park.

The Shenandoah Valley lies between this crest and the Allegheny and Shenandoah ranges to the west—the valley runs generally north-south. It was here that Stonewall Jackson gained immortality in his Civil War Valley Campaign. For four years, this was the "valley of humiliation" for Union forces, with Confederate armies in solid control of the strategic region. Stony Man Mountain, so called for the noble profile visible on its flank (see inside back cover), is one of the dominant features of this beautiful region. Hawks Bill Mountain, about ten miles due south of Stony Man, peaks at 4049 feet. Reddish Knob, far west-southwest in the Shenandoahs, has 4398 feet. From the Blue Ridge crest eastward, there is no comparable terrain.

ADVISORY
STONY MAN FARM:
Architecture and Landscape

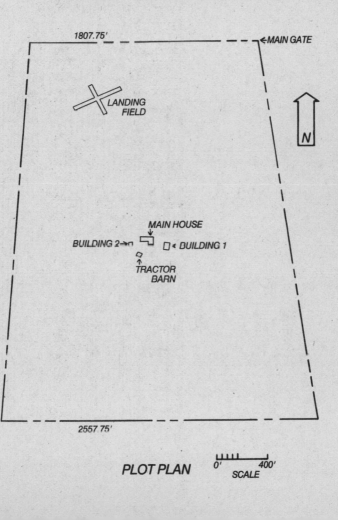

1807.75'   ← MAIN GATE

LANDING
FIELD

N

MAIN HOUSE
BUILDING 2 → ↓   □ ◄ BUILDING 1
↑
TRACTOR
BARN

2557.75'

PLOT PLAN   0'   400'
                       SCALE

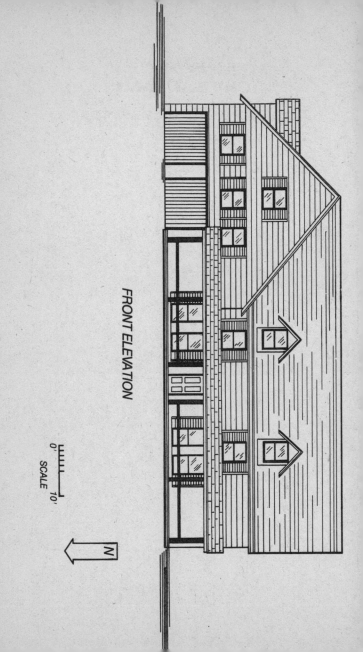

FRONT ELEVATION

SCALE
0' 10'

N

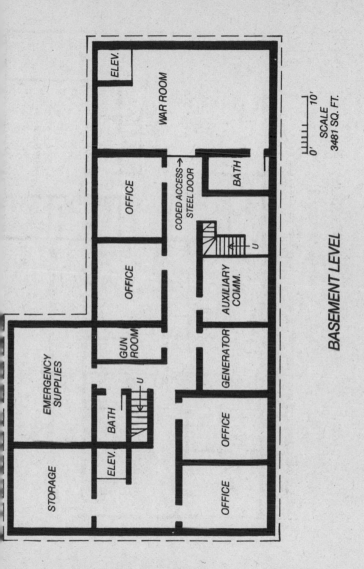

ELEV.

WAR ROOM

OFFICE

OFFICE

GUN
ROOM

EMERGENCY
SUPPLIES

STORAGE

CODED ACCESS →
STEEL DOOR

BATH

U

AUXILIARY
COMM.

GENERATOR

ELEV. BATH

U

OFFICE

OFFICE

SCALE
3481 SQ. FT.

0'   10'

BASEMENT LEVEL

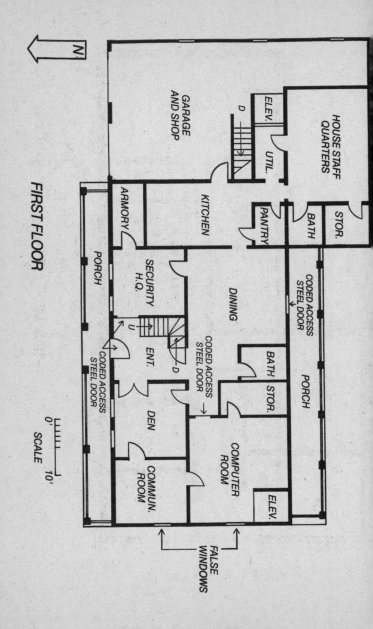

FIRST FLOOR

N

GARAGE
AND SHOP

HOUSE STAFF
QUARTERS

ELEV.

UTIL.

D

STOR.

BATH

PANTRY

KITCHEN

ARMORY

CODED ACCESS
STEEL DOOR

DINING

SECURITY
H.Q.

PORCH

PORCH

U

ENT.

D

CODED ACCESS
STEEL DOOR

CODED ACCESS
STEEL DOOR

BATH

STOR.

DEN

COMPUTER
ROOM

COMMUN.
ROOM

ELEV.

FALSE
WINDOWS

0'   10'
SCALE

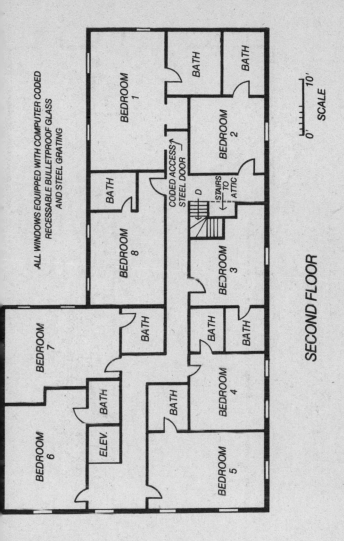

ALL WINDOWS EQUIPPED WITH COMPUTER CODED
RECESSABLE BULLETPROOF GLASS
AND STEEL GRATING

BEDROOM 1

BATH

BATH

BEDROOM 2

BATH

BEDROOM 8

CODED ACCESS
STEEL DOOR

STAIRS
TO
ATTIC

BEDROOM 3

BATH

BATH

BATH

BEDROOM 7

BATH

BEDROOM 4

BATH

ELEV.

BATH

BEDROOM 6

BATH

BEDROOM 5

SECOND FLOOR

0'   10'
SCALE

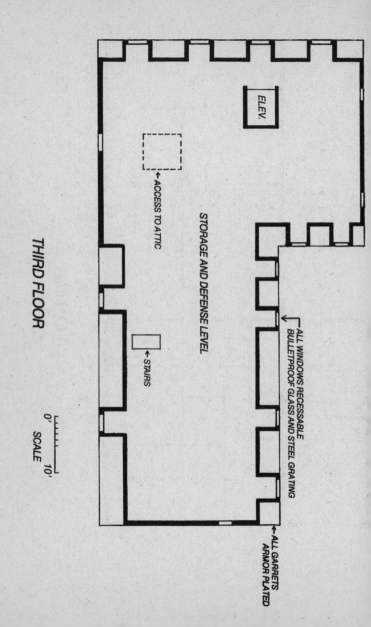

THIRD FLOOR

SCALE
0' 10'

STORAGE AND DEFENSE LEVEL

ELEV.

← ACCESS TO ATTIC

← STAIRS

← ALL WINDOWS RECESSABLE
BULLETPROOF GLASS AND STEEL GRATING

← ALL GARRETS
ARMOR PLATED

OUTBUILDING 1

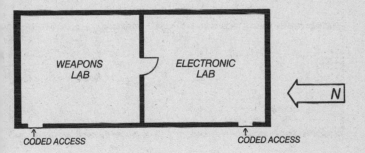

OUTBUILDING 2

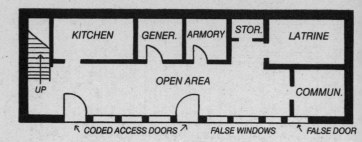

LEVEL ONE

OUTBUILDING 1

LEVEL TWO

0'   10'
SCALE

The Gallery

Presenting all the characters from

Mack Bolan #39–#62
Able Team #1–#9
Phoenix Force #1–#9
Stony Man Doctrine

Abbott, George—pirate atomic physicist heading Wei Ho's plutonium factory in remote regions of Brazil. *Amazon Slaughter*

Abdul—Lyons's taximan and battle ally against the Muslim Brotherhood. *Cairo Countdown*

Adamian, Marko—millionaire import-exporter of petro products and head of World Armenian Congress. Possessed by his Armenian cause, he buys a fighting force, Secret Liberation Army of Armenia, to strike a blow against Turkey. He is double-crossed by Paradine and held captive at the Turkish People's Liberation Army base. Rescued by Bolan, he joins in the blitz to destroy the heroin base. *Double Crossfire*

Aguilar, Evita "Eve"—undercover agent planted into middle echelon of Leonard Jericho's organization. Identity discovered, she is skinned alive by Santos the Butcher before Bolan can rescue her. A Bolan mercy kill. *Libya Connection*

Ahmad—Palestinian terrorist with Paradine. Beaten to death by Paradine after rape attempt on Sarah Shepherd. *Paradine's Gauntlet*

Alcantara, Roberto—illegitimate Colombian son of E.M. Davis and leader, power and money of Anthony Zuniga's terrorist takeover of WorldFiCor. Captured by Able Team and forced to aid in Able Team's assault of the hostaged tower. Killed as a traitor by Zuniga. *Tower of Terror*

Ali, Damu Abdul—a.k.a. Grover Jones, head of ambush squad hired by Al Miller. Using paramour Kelly Crawford as shield, Ali escapes but is later killed by Bolan. *Day of Mourning*

Allen, Professor—head of UN-Ford Foundation-funded American Economic Study group taken hostage by terrorists in Argentina. Rescued by Phoenix Force. *Argentine Deadline*

Alsado, Carmelita—sister of terrorist Luis Alsado. Sent word of the hostages, which led to their rescue by Phoenix Force. Killed by Luis Alsado. *Argentine Deadline*

Alsado, Luis—a.k.a. Martin. Argentine *estancia* owner and leader of terrorists posing as El Ejercito Revolucionario del Pueblo—ERP—kidnapped American Economic Study Group for economic gain and revenge for his bankruptcy. Killed by Keio Ohara. *Argentine Deadline*

Amal—a Tuareg tribesman and Rani's personal bodyguard around the club. A Bolan kill during raid. *Sold for Slaughter*

Anders, Tommy—born Giuseppe Androsepitone, popular stand-up comedian in U.S. and Europe. Undercover federal agent with the Justice Department's Sensitive Operations Group. *Renegade Agent*

Arness, Col. Matthew—U.S. Army Intelligence, USAEUR Sector working with the BND, NATO Security, GSG-9 and Phoenix Force investigating the killings of U.S. Army personnel. *Ultimate Terror*

Avancini, Fred—chief engineer for Trans-Alaska pipeline and inside man for INLA's assault against Prudhoe Pumping Station. *White Hell*

Avanquilla, Julio—President of Buenaventura Transportation Co. of Colombia and owner of Nivea Shipping and Condor Airlines, all used to smuggle Tiger Enterprises heroin into the U.S. A Bolan kill. *Tiger War*

Ballard, Colonel—Commander of Red Bluff Arsenal, drugged and forced to aid Red Anvil terrorists in seizing Dessler Laser Submachine Guns. To save Keio Ohara from the colonel's zombied kill squad, McCarter kills Colonel Ballard. *Atlantic Scramble*

Bambabele, Andrew—former first prime minister of Kuranda, exiled in Canada, apparently organizing his eventual return to power. Requisitions Bolan's aid in retrieving diamonds and secret documents from Brendan Scarr and KGB. Steals diamonds on Bolan's return, attempts escape. A Bolan kill in a precharged car. *Ambush on Blood River*

Banjo, Royce—outlaw country-and-western singer sympathetic to the Weather Underground cause to the point of hiding terrorist leader J.D. Dante. Captured by Bolan and April and told of Dante's murderous plot, including his own death, at the OPON Festival, he aids Bolan with information leading to the terrorists. *Flesh Wounds*

Barnes-Fenwick, Clifford—Welsh Olympic archer kidnapped by Zwilling Horde. Rescued by Bolan. *Bloodsport*

Battaglia, Benny—Kansas mafioso and white slaver, supplying kidnapped women for a Middle East slave market. A Bolan kill. *Sold for Slaughter*

Bensabat, Christian—president of Bensabat Investment Co., Beirut. Responsible for investing Tiger Enterprises income from U.S. heroin sales. A Bolan kill. *Tiger War*

Benson, Sally—a.k.a. Allison Dubin, undercover federal agent, infiltrated Weather Underground. Her identity is discovered, and she is rescued by Bolan. *Flesh Wounds*

Blackwell, Gen. Jeremiah—a.k.a. Blood Doctor. Leader of the Black Cobras with delusions of becoming the King of Africa via the destruction of the Aswan Dam. To avenge the degradation and death of Nemtala, Blackwell's death is saved for Phoenix Force's Gary Manning and his H&K. *Aswan Hellbox*

Blancanales, Rosario—from a Chicano background, he's known as "Pol" for Politician. Moves like a native, no matter where he is. Understands the enemy, then either changes him or neutralizes him. A hero of Able Team.

Blancanales, Toni—sister of Rosario Blancanales. Beaten and raped by psycho rapist-murderer Courtney Gilman. Abducted by Danny Toppacardi to silence her. Rescued by Bolan and Rosario. *The Violent Streets*

Blau, Rudi—strong-arm goon of Zwilling Horde. A Bolan kill. *Bloodsport*

Bohler, Col. Ludwig—Grenzschutzgruppe-neun—GSG-9—agent working with BND, U.S. Army Intelligence, NATO Security Forces and Phoenix Force investigating the killings of U.S. Army personnel. *Ultimate Terror*

Bolan, Mack—alias John Macklin Phoenix, retired colonel, U.S.A., a.k.a. Kicker, Striker, Stony Man One, also known at one time or another by the following aliases: Mike Blanski, Phil Tarrantino, Frankie Vinton, Stephen Ruggi, Mike Borzi, B. Macklin, Sergeant

Nalob, Harry Peterson, Omega, Stone, Michael Rideout, Nick. Mack Bolan is The Executioner.

Booth, Tommy—Nguyen Van Minh's chief of security. A Bolan kill. *Doomsday Disciples*

Breton, Harrison Payne—U.S. high-tech contractor, president and chief executive officer of Breton Industries, developers of Project Little Bang. Breton's daughter is kidnapped and he attempts a rescue, but he is captured and must be rescued himself by Bolan. *Terrorist Summit*

Breton, Jill Marie—daughter of Harrison Payne Breton, she is "out to save the world" with the Third World People's Liberation Front, but she is actually being held for ransom of a low-yield nuclear device. Rescued by Bolan twice, she becomes an ally in the final battle. *Terrorist Summit*

Brognola, Hal—director of Sensitive Operations Group, Stony Man liaison with the Oval Office. Third-generation American who worked his way into the stratosphere of the Justice Department's covert operations section. In that capacity he first met Mack Bolan.

Brown, Jimmy Lee—Bolan assailant at Interstate Loan Association ambush. Bolan shoots Brown's ear off and then follows him back to his hideout. A Bolan kill. *Day of Mourning*

Bruce, Holly—abducted daughter of Warco biochemist Dr. William Bruce. She is rescued by Bolan and becomes an ally of Bolan in her father's rescue. *Paramilitary Plot*

Bruce, Dr. William—biochemist and chief of biological research for energy conglomerate corporation Warco. Duped and coerced into developing virulént bubonic plague derivatives for paramilitary use. Rescued by Bolan. *Paramilitary Plot*

Brunow, Ilse—a German neo-Nazi with links to "old money" and high society in Western Europe, she supplies outlets for the slave-trade cartel's human merchandise. Killed by Smiley Dublin. *Sold for Slaughter*

Bryant, Sid—former FBI agent turned free-lance European and Mideast merc. Bolan captures Bryant, assumes identity to infiltrate Edward's operation. Bolan leaves Bryant in the desert for "a long walk home." *Renegade Agent*

Buckley, Chris—U.S. Congressman, devoted to investigating conspiracies and federal intrigues. Calls Able Team to intercede to protect reporter Floyd Jefferson and Rivera family against Roberto Quesada's death squad. *Justice by Fire*

Burger, Franz—formerly of Hitler's Youth Movement, smuggled out of Nazi stronghold in Paraguay and placed in a foreign country as ODESSA sleeper agent. Active agent for ODESSA allied with Baader-Meinhof gang to capture NATO 222 missile site. Killed by Phoenix Force. *Ultimate Terror*

Butterfield, Lou—FBI agent on special task force trailing gunrunners in Texas. Chased and murdered by gunners and left in the desert. *Warlord of Azatlan*

Cabelli, Gino—Raul Hernandez's third-in-command at Paradise Valley hardsite. Sara Williams saves Bolan by killing Cabelli. *Mountain Rampage*

Caceres, Sgt. Pedro—second-in-command in capture of Paraguayan terrorists and U.S. hostages. *Guerilla Games*

Cafferty, Bryan—second-in-command of Irish National Liberation Army. Killed by Phoenix Force. *White Hell*

Carlo—Lutfi's comrade from the Red Brigades. A Bolan kill is presumed. *Crude Kill*

Carter, Jon—Mafia Black Ace, sole survivor of the elite corps of mob assassins. Now bodycock and right-hand man to new Mafia don, Frank Contadina. In Bolan hellfire at Third World People's Liberation Army base camp, kills boss Contadina in his escape attempt. A Bolan kill. *Terrorist Summit*

Carter, Mitchell—born Mihail Kapetyan, son of Soviet defector. Corporate attorney with Universal Devotees. Killed by Nguyen Van Minh while making escape. *Doomsday Disciples*

Cartright, Rick—Kenlandport youth determined to find captive girlfriend Becky Devereaux and to see an end to the terrorists in their town. An ally of Bolan in the assault against Big Jim Lane's island stronghold. *Island Deathtrap*

Chama—leader of the Paraguayan terrorists holding U.S. hostages. Captured by the Paraguayan army. *Guerilla Games*

Chan, Sann—head of Wei Ho's personal guard. Fate unknown. *Amazon Slaughter*

Charon, Frederick Donald—president of DonCo. Traitor captured by American Intelligence agents selling a prototype missile-guidance system to Soviet agent. *Renegade Agent*

Charissa, Anna—wife of UN ambassador, kidnapped by Etalo Yareem's forces. Rescued by Bolan and assumes UN position of her murdered husband. *Vulture's Vengeance*

Charissa, John Leonard—U.S. ambassador to UN touring Panama. Killed in kidnap attempt. *Vulture's Vengeance*

Ciucci, Ferdinando—Red Justice Column defector turned paid informer. Executed by former compatriots in Red Justice Column trap. *Tuscany Terror*

Clayton, Jeff—ex-Green Beret, operator of Toronto-based survivalcraft game and CP bar. Informs Manning of merc actions in Africa leading to Brendan Scarr. *Ambush on Blood River*

Clune, Liam—lieutenant of Seamus Riley's Army of the People's Republic of Ireland. Captured by Phoenix Force, he supplies information under cooperative witness act. *The Fury Bombs*

Coakley, Cavan—lieutenant of Seamus Riley. Fate unknown, but presumed dead. *The Fury Bombs*

Cohen, Prof. Milton—representative of Nuclear Research and Development Administration investigating with Phoenix Force the assaults on U.S. nuclear-power plants. *Tigers of Justice*

Collins, Maj. Joseph—U.S. Air Force C-130 pilot forced by threats to his family and crew held hostage to aid Seamus Riley and his Irish Raiders in the procurement of four air-launched cruise missiles. Killed in a plane crash caused by Riley. *The Fury Bombs*

Commacho, Bernardo—FALN soldier, leads Blancanales to FALN commander. *Tower of Terror*

Connie—Reno dancer, hired as window dressing for a two-man hit team ambushing Bolan in Nevada desert. Bolan returns her to civilization. *Brothers in Blood*

Conrad, Terry—photographer for Intercontinental Systems Ltd., taken hostage by Paraguayan terrorists. Manages to escape, and thinking he is rescued by Paraguayan army, returns to camp to be killed by soldiers. *Guerilla Games*

Contadina, Frank—new breed of Mafia don, building an alliance with international terrorism through Luke Harker's Third World People's Liberation Army summit. During Bolan blitz, Contadina's bodycock Jon Carter tries to save himself and kills Contadina. *Terrorist Summit*

Copa, Benny—a.k.a. Benjamin Copacetti, mafioso small guy used by Smalley for low-level gunning. A Bolan kill. *The Violent Streets*

Crawford, Ret. Brig. Gen. James—Bolan's commanding officer in Vietnam and the guiding light behind the Stony Man operation. *Day of Mourning*

Crawford, Kelly—daughter of General Crawford. Taken to living on the dangerous side with hired gun Grover Jones a.k.a. Damu Abdul Ali. When Ali's goons fail at an ambush, they are tracked by Bolan back to Ali's hideout where Bolan rescues Kelly and returns her to her father. *Day of Mourning*

Culp, Amy—Senator's daughter, rescued by Bolan from Universal Devotees. *Doomsday Disciples*

Daito—born Masaaki Sakade. Raised on hatred for America. Former commander of Japanese Red Army group. After plastic surgery and name change, serves as Edward Oshimi's lieutenant in Japanese Red Cell. Honoring the code of Bushido, Keio Ohara kills Daito in blade-against-blade samurai combat. *Dragon's Kill*

Dante, J.D.—renegade Weather Underground in alliance with Moscow's international terrorism. Working with Fyodor Zossimov in a plan to annihilate a country-and-western festival with napalm rain. Bolan mercy kills Dante, who had been trapped in the bowels of a rotating stage, but leaves corpse to be ground by the cogs. *Flesh Wounds*

Datcher, Sam—one of Damu Abdul Ali's goons sent to ambush Bolan at the Interstate Loan Association stakeout. The ambush fails, and Bolan follows the hit team back to their headquarters. A Bolan kill. *Day of Mourning*

Davis, Chris—Catalina Island teen resistance fighter against Outlaw motorcycle gang. *The Hostaged Island*

Davis, E.M.—president of World Financial Corporation. Conspiring with Puerto Rico Nationals in takeover-ransom plot of WorldFiCor tower to hide his $1 billion embezzlement earmarked for the purchase of a country for terrorist son Roberto Alcantara. *Tower of Terror*

Davis, Roger—Catalina Island teen, cousin of Chris Davis. Also joined in resistance fighting against motorcycle gang. *The Hostaged Island*

Dawson, Sandra—American student studying Japanese Jonin society firsthand, trying to connect past society with present-day Yakuza. Rescued more than once by Bolan before finally becoming a valuable ally. *Invisible Assassins*

Delaney, George "Horse"—leader of the Outlaws motorcycle gang in the Catalina Island takeover. Killed by the townspeople in revolt. *The Hostaged Island*

DeLuccia, Tom "The Weasel"—New Jersey mobster and Benny Battaglia's East Coast connection with buyers on the Continent and North Africa for slave merchandise. A Bolan kill, but not before he reveals his connections in Algiers. *Sold for Slaughter*

Dembo—crippled Munzoga street urchin witness to Ashwar Fawzi's traitor-for-hire deeds. Leads Phoenix Force to Fawzi. As reward, he is financially secure for life by Phoenix Force. *Aswan Hellbox*

Demura, Lieutenant—Kompei agent captured by the Japanese Red Cell and subjected to Prof. Yiochi's EES-brain-draining interrogation. Killed in fight to escape. *Dragon's Kill*

Deo Roi—Meo guerilla. Because of jealousy, he imperils Bolan's mission and escape, but allies with Bolan and Meo tribesmen for final assault. *Return to Vietnam*

DeRosa, Capt. Angel—Cuban advisor assigned to Gen. Blackwell and the Black Cobra. Fate unknown. *Aswan Hellbox*

DeSilva, Jesus—leader of terrorist diving operation recovering sunken nuclear device. A Bolan kill. *Day of Mourning*

Devane, Coletta "Collie"—the blood and gristle of the Irish National Liberation Army and paramour of topkick Sean Toolan. Killed by Yakov Katzenelenbogen. *White Hell*

Devereaux, Becky—kidnapped by Wilmer Moore for blackmail. Rescued by Rick Cartright and Bolan. *Island Deathtrap*

Deveraux, Tom—Kenlandsport fisherman blackmailed into running contraband for Becky's abductor. *Island Deathtrap*

DiAlto, Col. Mike—aide to the chief of staff for logistics and administration in NATO's Southern Command, and chief American liaison officer to the NOCS. Wife and daughter kidnapped by Red Justice Column. Joined Bolan in rescue of hostages and destruction of Column. *Tuscany Terror*

Diaz, Luisa—Puerto Rican National terrorist at WorldFiCor takeover. An Able Team kill. *Tower of Terror*

Dickman, Laurence—British major stationed in Belfast, tapped as liaison to Phoenix Force in searching for IRA's O'Bannon and captive McCarter. *The Fury Bombs*

Dieter, Ricardo—bastard son of former SS officer. ODESSA agent in charge of hit team assaulting missile-control center. Killed by Keio Ohara. *Ultimate Terror*

Dobbins, Harold—economics expert for Intercontinental Systems, hostage of Paraguayan terrorists. Rescued by Phoenix Force. *Guerilla Games*

Dolan, Clancy—Irish National Liberation Army soldier and one-time toy of Coletta Devane. Killed by Yakov Katzenelenbogen. *White Hell*

Doyle—American merc and second-in-command of Leonard Jericho's Libya hardsite. A Bolan kill. *Libyan Connection*

Drummond, Sir Philip—high-ranking British Intelligence officer and double agent for KGB. Captured by U.S. Intelligence buying

U.S. guidance systems for Soviets. Opted to inform in exchange for the protection of life imprisonment. *Renegade Agent*

Dublin, Smiley—one-time Ranger Girl and Bolan love interest. Federal undercover agent with the SOG. *Sold for Slaughter*

Dunlop, Stuart—undercover FBI agent probing Dr. William Bruce's disappearance. Killed via Warco's virulent bubonic plague. *Paramilitary Plot*

Dussault, Armand—top man in slave cartel, a Corsican thug who had prospered in the flesh trade. A Bolan kill. *Sold for Slaughter*

Echeverias, Rolando—Colonel Deputy Prefect of Police in charge of Criminal Investigation Division and liaison between Argentine security and Phoenix Force in the investigation of U.S. hostages. *Argentine Deadline*

Edwards, Frank—CIA agent turned renegade, trafficking with terrorists in Europe and Mideast. Creates an international underground intelligence network from top legitimate agencies to serve terrorists. Based in Libya and under the sponsorship of Khaddafi, the "black" CIA has near-governmental status. A Bolan kill. *Renegade Agent*

El Negro—Bolivia's warlord of the cocaine armies and south American ally of Tate Monroe. *Texas Showdown*

Encizo, Rafael—Cuban-American patriot. Survivor of Bay of Pigs and Castro's prisons. Expert in naval and underwater warfare, strong on leadership qualities. A hero of Phoenix Force.

Farnsworth, Lee—Central Foreign Bureau chief and opponent of Stony Man operation. *Day of Mourning*

Farrel, Emmett—a lieutenant of Seamus Riley's Irish Raiders. Captured by Phoenix Force. *The Fury Bombs*

Fawcett, Jack—lieutenant of homicide, protects psycho rapist-murderer Courtney Gilman for political gains. Goes straight, kills Smalley, the assistant police commissioner, who is behind the conspiracy. *The Violent Streets*

Fawzi, Ashwar—free-lance informer in Munzoga. Sells out Phoenix Force to Eritrean People's Liberation Front, leading to Gary Manning's capture and torture. Killed by David McCarter. *Aswan Hellbox*

Fedorenko, Kyashesla—designer and KGB power of Hydra. With the collapse of Hydra at hand, revenge-seeking Kinosuke Yoshida mutilates Fedorenko and leaves him to die. *Stony Man Doctrine*

Felipe—Luis Alsado's chief lieutenant. Injured in hand-to-hand combat with Keio Ohara, but spared. *Argentine Deadline*

Fenster, Jack—New York "laundryman" investing profits for Tiger Enterprises. Killed by Bolan's elephant. *Tiger War*

Fletcher, Deputy Sheriff Joseph—Avalon's deputy sheriff. Killed by Horse Delaney in takeover of Catalina Island. *The Hostaged Island*

Franks, Ed—Cornell agronomist and member of U.S. Economic Study Group, taken hostage by Luis Alsado. Rescued by Phoenix Force. *Argentine Deadline*

French, Roger—member of UN-Ford Foundation funded Economic group in Argentina taken hostage by Alsado and rescued by Phoenix Force. *Argentine Deadline*

Fujo Sakata—Osato Goro's lieutenant and second-in-command of Tigers of Justice. In charge of the organization's self-defense training program, he has aspirations of becoming a KGB SMERSH assassin. Killed in hand-to-hand combat with Keio Ohara. *Tigers of Justice*

Furst, Robert—commander of Tate Monroe's mercenary army. Previously arrested by Lyons, who was an LAPD detective, he knows Lyons is undercover, and Furst is recruited to help Able Team. Killed by Craig Pardee as traitor. *Texas Showdown*

Fusco, Niccola "Nicky"—Thurston Ward's connection to the Florida mob. One of the old mafiosi, a survivor of Bolan's Miami war. A Bolan kill. *Paramilitary Plot*

Gallucci, Agent—San Francisco-based agent for FBI and ally and agent for Colonel Quesada. Killed accidentally by Captain Madrano in ambush intended for the Rivera family. *Justice by Fire*

Ganz, Udo—German Olympic skier, kidnapped by the Zwilling Horde. Rescued by Bolan. *Bloodsport*

Garcia, Señora—coordinator in Department of Tourism and courier for Unomundo. Captured by Able Team, forced to guide them to Unomundo. Macheted by revenge-bent Luis. *Warlord of Azatlan*

Gargan, Charles—captain of hostage-rescue flight from Brazil, taken hostage by Paraguayan terrorists. Killed by terrorist leader Chama. *Guerilla Games*

Genet—Luis's chief lieutenant. Killed by Bolan in Monaco shoot-out. *Paradine's Gauntlet*

Ghazawi, Khader—founder and leader of Libya's Jeddah terrorist faction and its spin-off, Red Anvil. Killed by Yakov Katzenelenbogen, settling a vendetta from the Six Day War. *Atlantic Scramble*

Giancola, Pepsi—Mafia headcock at Interstate Loan Association ambush. A Bolan kill. *Day of Mourning*

Gilman, Courtney—son of Minnesota state legislator. Maniac rapist-murderer. Killed by Assistant Police Commissioner Smalley in Riverside Park. *The Violent Streets*

Grimaldi, Jack—combat pilot in Vietnam, later a flyboy for the Mob, became staunch Bolan ally, pilot for Stony Man. Can fly anything from a single-engine Scout to a Boeing 767. Bolan's ace weapon on many missions.

Gold, Phil—member of American Economics study group in Argentina, taken hostage by Luis Alsado. Rescued by Phoenix Force. *Argentine Deadline*

Gomez, Colonel—leader of Khmer Rouge slavers-traders, Cambodian mercs and Brazilian army patrols. Captured by Able Team to be returned to trial and justice by Lieutenant Silveres. *Amazon Slaughter*

Goro Giovanni—captain of the Red Brigades, attempts to take Bolan and the ransom in Chiasso. Presumed dead. *Paradine's Gauntlet*

Goro Osato—founder of pacifist antinuclear organization, Anzen Sekai, a cover for the Tigers of Justice, a vengeful terrorist *ninja* cult financed and supported by the KGB. As leader of the Tigers, he launches assaults against U.S. nuclear-power plants. Trapped in a nuclear containment room, he is doomed to die of radiation poisoning. *Tigers of Justice*

Gossage, Jennifer—financial vice-president for Intercontinental Systems, Ltd., taken hostage by Brazilian terrorists, Paraguayan terrorists and the Paraguayan army. Rescued by Phoenix Force. *Guerilla Games*

Green, Charlie—director of Eastern European Accounts for World Financial Corporation. Trapped in the tower during terrorist takeover, he organizes office defense and aids Able Team in gaining access to the tower and in the assault against the Puerto Rican Nationals. *Tower of Terror*

Grendal, Sgt. Edsel—U.S. soldier black-marketing U.S. Army weapons to Zwilling Horde. Killed by Bolan, who assumes his identity to infiltrate the terrorist group. *Bloodsport*

Gridell, Bob—CIA agent injured by Armenian terrorists at Interstate Loan Association ambush. Saved from death shot by Bolan. *Day of Mourning*

Grover, Donald—a.k.a. Mikhail Ivanovich Markov. Major in Soviet Komitet Gosudarstvennoy Bozopasnosti. Sleeper agent working as nuclear-plant inspector for EPA. Assigned as liaison to Tigers of

Justice. Killed by Phoenix Force's McCarter. *Tigers of Justice*

Gunther—ODESSA assassin. In a daylight attack of Ohara and Katzenelenbogen, Gunther is killed by the .22 Magnum finger of Katz's prosthetic hand. *Ultimate Terror*

Gurgen—Soviet adviser to South American terrorist coalition. *Day of Mourning*

Haddad, Jamal—former PLO member and aide to Yasser Arafat, he has since defected to form his own Palestinian People's Army, based in Algiers. Wounded during Bolan's blitz to rescue Smiley Dublin but allowed to live to carry an ultimatum to the slave cartel. *Sold for Slaughter*

Haddad, Khalid—Libyan sub commander transporting the Jeddah terrorists and stolen Dessler Laser Submachine Guns to Khaddafi. *Atlantic Scramble*

Hagen, Ella—wife of Richard Hagen, held hostage to ensure his cooperation. Tortured beyond reason, assumed a Bolan mercy kill. *Double Crossfire*

Hagen, Richard—born Dikran Hagopian. Private consultant, served as agent for Marko Adamian and Paradine. Double-crossed by Paradine, to be used as an embarrassment to the U.S. for his own supposed terrorist plotting. Held captive with Adamian at Turkish base. Rescued by Bolan and joins in battle against the Turkish People's Liberation Army. *Double Crossfire*

al-Haj, Rani—French Algerian operator of seedy Casbah nightclub which doubles as the Weasel's Algiers connection in the slave cartel. Killed as a "loose end" and potential threat by his own employers once the Bolan blitz begins. *Sold for Slaughter*

Hansen, T.W.—deserted from U.S. Special Forces to merc for Frank Edwards and the black CIA. A Bolan kill. *Renegade Agent*

Harker, Luke—hiding out in Algeria doing piece work for terrorists, Harker and Richard Wolfe create Third World People's Liberation Army, uniting terrorist groups and the new Mafia into a terrorist army for hire. A Bolan kill. *Terrorist Summit*

Harrington, Maj. Sam—Prudhoe Trans-Alaska Pipeline frontman and procurement officer, Phoenix Force liaison. *White Hell*

Harrison, Walt—old Vietnam buddy of Bolan's, now State Department agent. Killed by Lutfi. *Crude Kill*

Hatsumi—Japanese Red Cell technician and assistant to Professor Yiochi. Killed by Lieutenant Demura after having fatally wounded Demura. *Dragon's Kill*

Heath—cargo pilot shot down delivering supplies to Bolan. Joins in Bolan's operation against Tiger Enterprises. *Tiger War*

Heffernan, Cormick—leader in the council of the Provisional Irish Republican Army. Aids Phoenix Force in ferreting out Seamus Riley and his plans. *The Fury Bombs*

Hernandez, Raul—head of security at Paradise Valley hardsite. Killed in battle by well-placed shot to the gas tank by Bolan or Sara Williams. *Mountain Rampage*

Hershey, Bob—CIA agent, Cairo. Killed by Muslim Brotherhood in CIA assault on terrorist hideout. *Cairo Countdown*

Hirito—Tiger of Justice *ninja*. An Encizo kill. *Tigers of Justice*

Hoang, Pierce—merc watchman for Wei Ho, captured by Able Team and used to lead to Chan Sann. *Amazon Slaughter*

Hoffer, Klaus Erich—former Nazi clerk at Auschwitz, now ERP sympathizer. Killed by Rafael Encizo. *Argentine Deadline*

Hoffman, Allen "Tex"—bodycock and guard for Third World People's Liberation Army safehouse taken by Bolan and forced into an awkward alliance, aiding Bolan in and out of Harker's Third World base camp and providing backup. Killed by Rikki Roybal. *Terrorist Summit*

Hohlstrom—Israeli agent, infiltrated Leonard Jericho's operation as Swedish merc. Bolan battle ally, killed by Jericho's forces. *Libya Connection*

Holbein, Kurt—project director at Paradise Valley. Bolan shoots vial of HA27, and the contaminated shards inject Holbein with the liquid death. *Mountain Rampage*

Holt, David—San Francisco attorney representing Salvadoran ex-mayor Rivera and slain reporter Ricardo Marquez. Kidnapped and mutilated by Quesada's death squad. *Justice by Fire*

Holt, Kenneth—senior vice-president Intercontinental Systems, taken hostage by Paraguayan and Brazilian terrorists. Rescued by Phoenix Force. *Guerilla Games*

Horton, Al—agent on FBI special task force trailing gunrunners. Mutilated and left in Texas desert. *Warlord of Azatlan*

Horuk—a.k.a. Hook. Muslim conscript into TPLA. Spared by Bolan in an ambush, Hook pledges his allegiance to Bolan as comrade. Fights with Bolan and rescues hostages in the blitz on Paradine's heroin base. Killed by Paradine. *Double Crossfire*

Hoshiro Satsu—owner and manager of Hoshiro Company, headquarters for the Japanese Red Cell. Serving as Red Cell commander,

Hoshiro is killed in Phoenix Force probe of Hoshiro complex. *Dragon's Kill*

Hunnsecker, Otto—Nazi living in Argentina, recognizes Yakov Katzenelenbogen to be a Mossad agent and has him kidnapped. Killed by Keio Ohara. *Argentine Deadline*

ibn-Hassan, Ali—Algiers brothel keeper, prominent in local underworld. His establishment is leveled in Bolan's blitz to recover captive Smiley Dublin. Severely wounded, he disappeared, his fate unknown. *Sold for Slaughter*

Ibrahim, Abdel—counteragent in Munzoga, Phoenix Force contact. Killed by an Eritrean Liberation terrorist. *Aswan Hellbox*

Ikeda Ken—colonel, chief of Japanese Kompei Special Internal Affairs replacing the recently "retired with help from Colonel Phoenix," Nakada. Allied with Phoenix Force in operations against the Japanese Red Ceil terrorists. *Dragon's Kill*

Illyanovich, Ivan—KGB chief, posing as Soviet assistant cultural attaché in Belgrade. Masterminded plot to ambush Bolan at Udine. *Paradine's Gauntlet*

Izmir, Mustafa—gun for Armenian terrorist group, the Justice Commandos of Armenian Genocide. Killed by Bolan at Interstate Loan Association ambush. *Day of Mourning*

James, Corey—former CIA agent, working as chief of operations for Frank Edwards. Bolan amputates his arm with an Uzi blast but gains information to Edwards's hardsite. Bolan destroys the safehouse but leaves James in the clear. Fate unknown. *Renegade Agent*

Jefferson, Floyd "The Cat"—free-lance reporter trying to expose Roberto Quesada's Salvadoran death squads. Searches and fights alongside Able Team to defend the Rivera family. Wounded by death-squad goon, he recovers to join Able Team in the trenches in El Savador. *Justice by Fire, Kill School*

Jericho, Leonard "Lenny"—fugitive financier selling weapons to Shahkhia to support coup against Khaddafi. Bolan kills two lookalike Jerichos before he gets the real one. *Libya Connection*

Jessup, Clark—Phoenix Force liaison to White House and Pentagon. *White Hell*

Jibril, Bihar—topcock of the ELF in Munzoga and Blackwell's cohort in Aswan Dam plot. Captures Gary Manning and tortures him before a Phoenix Force rescue. Wounded, Jibril makes one final attempt to kill Manning but kills Nemtala instead. Manning, in an act of revenge and sorrow, beats Jibril to death. *Aswan Hellbox*

Kabrina—Kurd, heading a family rebellion against opium growing for Paradine's Turkish People's Liberation Army. Assists Bolan and ends up in the crossfire of Takim's hit squad and is taken captive. Rescued by Bolan, she fights at Bolan's side to destroy the TPLA heroin base. *Double Crossfire*

Kagor, Pete—Al Miller's second-in-command in the attack against Stony Man Farm. Kagor wounds Captain Wade, but is killed by Wade. *Day of Mourning*

Kagwa—corporal and second-in-command in Mumungo's Leopard Patrol. Killed by Katzenelenbogen. *Ambush on Blood River*

Kalinin, Alex—chemical-warfare officer in KGB. Killed by nerve gas in battle with Phalange commandos at a Bolan airstrip strike in northern Ireland. *Stony Man Doctrine*

Kambolo—Mussengamba tribesman, bush driver and battle ally for Bolan and Phoenix Force. Killed by Luke Rawson. *Ambush on Blood River*

Karpov, Viktor—KGB operative and covert liaison to Red Justice Column. A Bolan kill. *Tuscany Terror*

Katzenelenbogen, Yakov—French-Israeli, known as "Katz." Former intelligence chief, underground guerilla veteran. Right arm missing below elbow, casualty of Mideast wars. A hero of Phoenix Force.

Kearney, Girvin—Provos informant to whereabouts of McCarter when he was a hostage of O'Bannon. Served as go-between for Heffernan and Phoenix Force. *The Fury Bombs*

Kelsay, Mike—second-in-command of Irish National Liberation Army after death of Bryan Cafferty. Kelsay is assumed killed in Phoenix Force assault. *White Hell*

Kemal, Ismet—chief enforcer for Armenian terrorist group. Killed by Bob Gridell in CIA ambush at Interstate Loan Association. *Day of Mourning*

Kennedy—merc, head honcho at Leonard Jericho's villa operation in Bishabia. A Bolan kill. *Libya Connection*

Kerr, Johnny—young off-season manager of Tide Creek Lodge on Salmon River. A painful reminder of Johnny Bolan, Kerr proves to be a valuable Bolan ally. *Brothers in Blood*

Kirov, Yuri—colonel, highly placed KGB gopher attached to Russian terrorist branch, this Department *V.* Soviet engineer who supervised construction of the Aswan Dam also engineers its destruction via Blackwell's Nike Ajax missile. Fate unknown. *Aswan Hellbox*

with his "comrades" from the L.A. Youth Action Corporation. he finds they are drugged killer punks and is macheted to death. *Army of Devils*

Lansdale—head agent at Benghazi's covert CIA facility, the Mid-Am Incorporated. *Libya Connection*

Latchford, Bobby—down-on-luck Viet vet forced to enlist in Yareem's army. Found in jungle by Bolan, became allies to probe Yareem's encampment and rescue hostages. Rewarded with assignment to special Presidential Committee to aid and readjust Viet vets. *Vulture's Vengeance*

Laval—a racketeer and smuggler in southern France, dealing in drugs and weapons. A Bolan kill. *Paradine's Gauntlet*

La Vibora—a.k.a. "The Snake." Leader of Red Patrol, captain of the Popular Liberation Forces. Killed by former recruit, Ricardo. *Kill School*

Le Duc Trang—general, commander of Viet military prison and boss of Red River Delta heroin trade. A Bolan kill. *Return to Vietnam*

Lettieri, Vito—Goro's Red Brigades contact in Milan. Fate unspecified. *Paradine's Gauntlet*

Le Valle, Maurice—the "Great Man," the power and the money behind the mind-control research at the Paradise Valley hardsite. Killed in battle with Bolan and Kathy O'Connor. *Mountain Rampage*

Levesque, Donald—member of American Economic Study Group in Argentina, taken hostage by Luis Alsado. Rescued by Phoenix Force. *Argentine Deadline*

Lieter, Karl—general, West German Intel Organization, the Bundesnachrichtendienst—BND—working with U.S. Army Intel, NATO Security Forces, GSG-9 and Phoenix Force investigating the killings of U.S. Army personnel. *Ultimate Terror*

Ling Ty—Col. Liu Hsaio's daughter, aided by Bolan in escape from Tiger Enterprises hardsite. She is captured by Shan Liberation Army to be their doctor, but is rescued by Bolan. *Tiger War*

Liu Hsaio—vicious and ruthless president of Tiger Enterprises. Killed in ceremonial combat by Bolan. *Tiger War*

Lizco, Alfred—captain, Democratic Liberation Front. Leads DLF guerillas in assault against Roberto Quesada's Honduran kill school with Able Team. *Kill School*

Lizco, Guillermo—younger brother of Alfred Lizco and lieutenant of Las Boinas Negras, the Black Berets. Seeking revenge and justice for the death of his family and fellow Salvadoran countrymen, sets up information to capture Quesada for trial in U.S., but Quesada escapes. Allies with Able Team in assault on Quesada's hardsite. *Kill School*

Lobato, Jesse—bodycock for Big Jim Lane. A Bolan kill. *Islan Deathtrap*

Logan, Peter—brigadier general, Army Intelligence. Representativ at top-secret conference of American and Japanese intelligenc officers. Killed by Red Cell terrorists. *Dragon's Kill*

Lopez, Miguel—merc guard for Wei Ho, captured by Able Team leads them to Chan Sann. *Amazon Slaughter*

Lopez, Jorge—El Rojo's second-in-command, revolution organize and liaison between El Rojo and Monroe's merc army. Assume killed with Rojo in Grimaldi air strike. *Texas Showdown*

Louis—ranking leader of Unione Corse—Corsican syndicate—i France. Attempts to intercept Bolan and the ransom in Monaco. *A* Bolan kill. *Paradine's Gauntlet*

Luis—Dr. Orozco's antifascist, revenge-seeking resistance fighte Leads Able Team to Unomundo's couriers. Killed by Unomundo goons. *Warlord of Azatlan*

Lutfi—international terrorist with plot of atomic terrorism. Die when directly exposed to an enriched-uranium fuel rod. *Crude Kil*

Lynch, Tom—Irish National Liberation Army soldier. Assume killed by Phoenix Force. *White Hell*

Lynch, Detroit—Weather Underground terrorist and henchman fo J.D. Dante. A Bolan kill. *Flesh Wounds*

Lyons, Carl—Blond, blue-eyed ex-LAPD sergeant, veteran of th Justice Dept.'s war against organized crime, a fear-inspiring be serker, full of smooth motion and sudden explosions of energy. *A* pack horse too, because of insistence on taking along the righ equipment. "Ironman" to those who know him. A hero of Abl Team.

MacGrew, Doyle—Riley's lieutenant in assault on Army of th People's Republic of Ireland hideout. Captured by Phoenix Force *The Fury Bombs*

MacMurray, Donald—inspector, Royal Ulster Constabulary, liaiso to Phoenix Force in locating Riley, O'Bannon and McCarter captors. *The Fury Bombs*

Madigan, Betty—agriculturist from UC, Davis, member of UN-For Foundation-funded American Economic Study Group taken hostag by terrorist Luis Alsado. *Argentine Deadline*

Madrano, Alejandro—captain   Organización   Democrátic

Nacionalista—ORDEN. Leader of a death squad searching for investigative reporter Jefferson and his protectors, Able Team. Killed by Able Team in ambush planned for them. *Justice by Fire*

Malakesi—former minister of justice of Kuranda under Prime Minister Bambabele. Now in exile in Canada serving as Bambabele's aid. Disillusioned by Bambabele's betrayal, steps in front of Bambabele's gun and is killed. *Ambush on Blood River*

Mandone, Manny—Mafia shark, now strong arm for Leonard Jericho's operation in the Bahamas. A Bolan kill. *Libya Connection*

Manning, Gary—Canadian. Ballistics, explosives and security engineer. Counterterrorism investigator, Special Forces instructor. Rugged, strong, fast. A hero of Phoenix Force.

Marchado, Pete—drug runner under surveillance for contact with Tate Monroe's Texas Irregulars. Killed in drug robbery, and Rosario Blancanales assumes his identity to infiltrate Monroe's operations. *Texas Showdown*

Maria—Nicaraguan teen, serves as guide and backup for Able Team recon and destruction of Hydra base. Wounded by Hydra terrorists. *Stony Man Doctrine*

Marquez, Ricardo—Latin American correspondent for *San Francisco Globe* reporting from El Salvador. Beheaded and mutilated by Roberto Quesada's death squad, El Ejercito de los Guerreras Blancos. *Justice by Fire*

Martella, Antonio—Red Justice Column leader and crew boss. Fingered by Leo Turrin as a CIA agent, a traitor to the Column. Killed by Karpov. *Tuscany Terror*

Mashir, Ahmad—Khatib's chief interrogator. A Bolan kill. *The New War*

McCarter, David—British. Anti-terror, riot control and commando expert. Former SAS officer. Rude, cynical. Sharp sense of humor. A hero of Phoenix Force.

McFee, Robert—colonel, Military Intelligence liaison with CIA and old Bolan comrade from Vietnam days. Stayed behind at end of the war to fight with the Meos and search for U.S. POWs. Captured and tortured by Viet military. Rescued by Bolan and survives despite severe injuries. *Return to Vietnam*

Merida, Captain—federally assigned liaison and guide for Able Team. Leads them directly into Unomundo's death-squad ambush. Captured by Able Team and executed by Guatemalan government as traitor. *Warlord of Azatlan*

Merrill, Thomas—lieutenant-colonel U.S. Army, assigned to S-1

Department of Intelligence stationed in South Korea as cryptographer. Murdered by Red Cell assassins. *Dragon's Kill*

Michael—American merc, Paradine's lieutenant. Fate unspecified
but presumed killed in Bolan's final blitz. *Paradine's Gauntlet*

Miller, Al—merc gone bad. Head of commando-training camp and
leader of the attack on Stony Man Farm. Killed by Wade. *Day of
Mourning*

Miller, Muriel—PR rep for Intercontinental Systems Ltd., taken
hostage by Brazilian terrorists, Paraguayan terrorists and Paraguayan army. Tortured by Paraguayan terrorist leader Chama.
Rescued by Phoenix Force. *Guerilla Games*

Mohammed—Able Team assistant, interpreter and battle ally in Cairo
operation against Muslim Brotherhood. *Cairo Countdown*

Minera—poses as head of Eshan Nazarour's security force, but is
Arnesto "Arnie the Farmer" Castiglione's heir, striking a new deal
with the Mafia and the Mideast for nukes. A Bolan kill. *Iranian Hit*

Monet, Claude—bomb maker and explosives expert imported into
the U.S. by Big Jim Lane. A Bolan kill. *Island Deathtrap*

Monroe, Availa—Tate Monroe's wife, Rojo's sister. Killed in Grimaldi air strike of Texas Irregulars hardsite. *Texas Showdown*

Monroe, Tate—dying Texas billionaire using last days to buy merc
army to assassinate the president of Mexico. Killed in Grimaldi air
strike. *Texas Showdown*

Moore, Elsa—elderly woman nabbed from a Denver rest home and
used for medical experiments at Paradise Valley. Killed by Lavinia
Vitalli and Formula HA27. *Mountain Rampage*

Moore, Wilmer—Kenlandsport fisherman. Abducted Becky Devereaux to blackmail Tom Deveraux into hauling contraband for him.
Wounded by Moore victim Bud Stiles and fed to the pigs by Becky's
relatives. *Island Deathtrap*

Morales, Colonel—federally assigned liaison for Able Team and also
leader of Unomundo's death squad assigned to hit Able Team.
Captured by Able and executed by Guatemalan government as
traitor. *Warlord of Azatlan*

Morganslicht, Tanya—co-leader with twin brother, Thomas, of
Zwilling Horde. Killed by Thomas. *Bloodsport*

Morganslicht, Thomas—co-leader of Zwilling Horde. A Bolan kill.
Bloodsport

Mugunga, Salibogo—Kababish tribesman from Black Cobra-
destroyed village, Abu Darash. To avenge murder of family and
conscription of son and daughter, Nemtala, Mugunga joins search

for Blackwell. Becomes trusted and beloved ally and friend. *Aswan Hellbox*

Mulanda—Mussengamba tribesman, bush driver and battle ally of Bolan and Phoenix Force. *Ambush on Blood River*

Müller, Heinrich—formerly of Hitler Youth Movement, lieutenant in SS. ODESSA commander allied with Baader-Meinhof faction to take control of NATO 222 missile site and blackmail U.S. and USSR out of Germany. Killed by Rafael Encizo in raid on ODESSA headquarters. *Ultimate Terror*

Mumungo, General—power behind puppet king of Kuranda. Killed in plane crash while doing recon of Bolan battle. *Ambush on Blood River*

Munoz y Villamor, Jorge—officer in the Dirreción General de Inteligencia—DGI—of the People's Republic of Cuba. Leader of Hydra responsible for supplying chemicals and weapons for Hydra project. During the Stony Man attack of Hydra's island, Munoz attempts to escape and is killed aboard boats precharged by Stony Man forces. *Stony Man Doctrine*

Murray, Dan—captain, U.S. Army stationed at Prudhoe Pumping Station, working as inside man for Irish National Liberation Army. Ushered Coletta Devane and her sabotage vanguard into the Alaskan pipeline pumping complex. Killed by Keio Ohara. *White Hell*

Mustaffa, Assad—oil-rich Saudi and number two in the slave-trade cartel providing money and a funnel for captives to the brothels of the Arab sheiks. Killed by Armand Dussault. *Sold for Slaughter*

Mwenkango—captain and leader of General Mumungo's personal bodyguards, the Leopard Patrol. Killed by Ziemba. *Ambush on Blood River*

Nakada, Commander Kingoro—head of security of Japanese National Police Agency. Groomed by *Kuma-kumi* to infiltrate agency. A Bolan kill. *Invisible Assassins*

Naramoto, Prof. Saburo—scientist for Red Sun Chemical Company. Believed lost in boating accident, found as hostage at Shoki Castle developing gas gangrene strain Anthrax B. Rescued by Bolan. *Invisible Assassins*

Nark—CIA agent posing as KGB operative. Taken hostage by Tiger Enterprises army. Rescued by Bolan, becomes battle ally. *Tiger War*

Nasaki—Tigers of Justice *ninja*, killed in hand-to-hand combat by Keio Ohara. *Tigers of Justice*

Naseer, Soraya—female Lebanese terrorist, ally and lover of Khatib al-Suleiman. Becomes grudging Bolan ally and helps Bolan rescue

Laconia. After mission's conclusion, goes on Mexican R&R with Grimaldi. *The New War*

Nate—ex-Marine fighting Unomundo's Nazi terrorism in Quiche. Leads Able Team and Mayan antifascist fighters against Unomundo's cavern fortress. *Warlord of Azatlan*

Navarro—ex-lieutenant working for El Rojo in tracking down Able Team infiltration of Monroe's Texas Irregulars. Shot down by Craig Pardee's troops but survives to reveal the agents within the ranks of Pardee. *Texas Showdown*

Nazarour, Carol—General Nazarour's wife, rescued by Bolan. *Iranian Hit*

Nazarour, Gen. Eshan—former high-ranker in Shah's SAVAK until revolution forced him into exile in U.S. Marked for assassination by Khomeini's paramilitary commando unit. Protected by Bolan from Iranian kill squad. Grimaldi strikes his departing plane. *Iranian Hit*

Nazarour, Dr. Medhi—brother and physician of General Nazarour. Warned Bolan of traitor element within Nazarour camp. Killed by Abbas Rafsanjani. *Iranian Hit*

Nemtala—daughter of Salibogo Mugunga, captured during Blackwell's raid on village of Abu Darash and forced into sexual servitude by Blackwell and Major Ochogilo. Makes her escape killing Ochogilo and joins Phoenix Force and father in destruction of Blackwell. Nemtala dies taking Bihar Jibril's knife intended for her lover, Gary Manning. *Aswan Hellbox*

Newton, Gravity—boxer and "station master" for Radical Express. Passes along necessary information for next station in Bolan's search for J.D. Dante. *Flesh Wounds*

Newton, Jake—Cairo-based CIA agent captured and beaten by Muslim Brotherhood. Rescued from National Liberation Front desert fortress by Able Team. *Cairo Countdown*

Nguyen Van Minh—founder and leader of the Universal Devotees. A Bolan kill. *Doomsday Disciples*

Nguyen Vinh—civilian liaison at military prison to check on General Trang's activities. Spared by Bolan for his pleas of mercy on behalf of Colonel McFee and for the information leading to McFee's rescue. *Return to Vietnam*

Nosenko, Uri—Soviet assassin working for KGB in coordinating the ambush at Udine. A Bolan kill. *Paradine's Gauntlet*

O'Bannon, Eamon—IRA leader and pal of Seamus Riley. Captured Phoenix Force's McCarter. Killed by Rafael Encizo in assault on abandoned church stronghold to rescue McCarter. *The Fury Bombs*

Ochogilo, Maj. Chilufia—Black Cobra's second-in-command and right arm of General Blackwell. Killed by Nemtala during his sexual assault. *Aswan Hellbox*

O'Connor, Kathy—teen hitchhiker abducted and held hostage for sexual use and medical experiments at Paradise Valley. Rescued by Bolan to become comrade-in-arms in destruction of hardsite. *Mountain Rampage*

O'Connor, Col. Theodore—USAEUR NATO Security Forces, works with BND, GSG-9, U.S. Army Intelligence and Phoenix Force, to investigate terrorist attacks against U.S. Army personnel. Killed by ODESSA agent Rudolf Kortze. *Ultimate Terror*

Ohara, Keio—Japanese martial arts and electronics expert, paracommando training. Tall for an Oriental, has complete knockout potential in one-on-one combat. A hero of Phoenix Force.

Okawa Akira—scientist heading research and development team of gas gangrene for Biotech Industries. Committed suicide over guilt for his involvement. *Invisible Assassins*

Oshimi, Prof. Edward—mastermind of Japanese Red Cell, the particle-beam projector and the New Empire of Japan. Killed by Rafael Encizo in Phoenix Force assault on Oshimi castle. *Dragon's Kill*

O'Reilly, Murph—Big Jim Lane's faithful cur. Died in Bolan blaze trying to save Lane. *Island Deathtrap*

O'Rourke, Peter—Seamus Riley lieutenant, captured by Phoenix Force. *The Fury Bombs*

Orozco, Doctor—leader of antifascist Guatemalan fighters opposing Unomundo. *Warlord of Azatlan*

Palmer, Aaron—deputy director of CIA captured by Daito and his Japanese Red Cell comrades. Interrogated by Professor Oshimi on EES brain-drain machine. Rescued by Phoenix Force in assault on Oshimi castle. *Dragon's Kill*

Paradine—international free-lance merc dealing in suit-to-order terrorism. Under contract to KGB to advise the Turkish People's Liberation Army in heroin producing-smuggling cadre. His operation is destroyed by Bolan. Seeking revenge, Paradine returns to hijack an airliner of diplomats for ransom. Paradine demands Bolan be the deliveryman. A Bolan kill. *Double Crossfire, Paradine's Gauntlet*

Pardee, Craig—recruiter for Monroe's Texas Irregulars. Recruits undercover Able Team as mercs. When their identity is known, Pardee leads merc forces against Able Team. Killed by Able Team. *Texas Showdown*

Parks, Craig—acting chief officer of Special Operations, CIA,

Cairo. Liaison to Yakov Katzenelenbogen, posing as foreign-service agent. *Cairo Countdown*

Pavloski, Babette—defected Czechoslovakian Olympic gymnast kidnapped by Zwilling Horde. Upon rescue by Bolan, she allies with Bolan for final siege. *Bloodsport*

Paxton, Bob—expatriate American, recruiting guards and soldiers for exiled conservative politicians and retired military officers. Identifies and tracks Able Team to El Negro and Pardee. Wounded when shot down with Navarro by Texas Irregular mercs. *Texas Showdown*

Perkins—CIA agent, London office. *Crude Kill*

Pornov, General—KGB agent directing Ahmad Shahkhia's coup against Khaddafi. Killed by Shahkhia. *Libya Connection*

Pouyan, Amir—Karim Yazid's second-in-command of Iranian hit team. A Bolan kill. *Iranian Hit*

Prescott, Robert—legal researcher for U.S. Congressman Buckley. As agent for Colonel Quesada, supplied him with information and assassins. Captured by Able Team and forced to trade information for safety. *Justice by Fire*

Quesada, Roberto—commander of El Ejercito de los Guerreros Blancas, El Salvador's death squad. Quesada lives in protection and luxury in Miami until Able Team makes it too hot. Forced to retreat to International Alliance stronghold in El Salvador. When pursued, forced to escape Able Team's wrath to Honduras with Unomundo. *Justice by Fire, Kill School*

Rafael—leader of El Ejercito Revolucionario del Peublo—ERP—in Córdoba. Leads Phoenix Force's Rafael Encizo into ambush, leaving him for dead. Killed by Encizo. *Argentine Deadline*

Rafsanjani, Abbas—General Nazarour's secretary, assistant and traitor to Nazarour regime. A Bolan kill. *Iranian Hit*

Ramón—leader of New York FALN group, supplied Blancanales with information regarding terrorists in WorldFiCor tower takeover. *Tower of Terror*

Randisi—backup for Phoenix Force in assault of Edward Oshimi's castle. Launched thermite-charged-warhead attack against castle remains. *Dragon's Kill*

Ranger, Toby—beautiful covert Fed, lately of Justice Department's Sensitive Operations Group. *Renegade Agent*

Rawson, Luke—surveyor for mining consortium, guide in tracking Brendan Scarr for Bolan team. Traitor, having made deal with Bambabele. A Bolan kill. *Ambush on Blood River*

Redfern, Matt—leader of Grey Dog, a splinter faction of the Irish

National Liberation Army. Out to blow up Seattle's oil-transfer terminals of Trans-Alaska pipeline. Killed by McCarter and Phoenix Force. *White Hell*

Reed, Harrison—representative from Nuclear Regulatory Commission investigating terrorist assaults on U.S. nuclear-power plants. *Tigers of Justice*

Revill, Ian—second officer of hostage-rescue plane from Brazil. Forced down by Paraguayan terrorists but escapes being taken hostage by Paraguayan army. Severely wounded by terrorist leader Chama. Rescued by Phoenix Force, allies in rescue of other hostages. *Guerilla Games*

el-Riadh, Omar—commander of National Liberation Front. Wounded by self-detonated fragmentation grenade and saved for interrogation by Able Team. *Cairo Countdown*

Ricardo—forced recruit of the Reds in Salvador. Captured in a firefight by Able Team. For reward of plane ticket and visa to U.S., leads Lyons and Blancanales against a Salvadoran death squad and Roberto Quesada's terrorists. *Kill School*

Rideout, Michael—CIA agent "retired" by Senate investigation, recruited by Leonard Jericho. Detained by CIA in Benghazi for Bolan to assume identity for infiltration of Jericho's forces. *Libya Connection*

Riley, Seamus—former ISRA—Irish Socialist Republican Army— soldier, found it too restrained. Organized and led the Army of the People's Republic of Ireland. A fight to the death between Riley and Gary Manning becomes a fight for life as Manning uses Riley as a shield in a leap from burning hideout. Riley is killed in the landing. *The Fury Bombs*

Riordan, Neal—Eamon O'Bannon's brother-in-law, supplying safehouse and passage into U.S. for Riley and vanguard. Phoenix Force follows Riordan to hideout, he is assumed captured with other Riley lieutenants in the raid. *The Fury Bombs*

Ritter, Heinz—son of ODESSA member. Ritter is double agent of SSD—Staats-Sicherheits-Dienst, East German State Security Service. An iron-curtain intel network agent supervised and manipulated by KGB, he works undercover with ODESSA agents and Baader-Meinhof faction in takeover of NATO missile site. Commits suicide when mission to alter missiles to West German targets could not be programmed. *Ultimate Terror*

Rivera, Antonio—former mayor from province of Sonsonate, El Salvador. Hiding in San Diego, self-exiled to U.S. after Quesada sends death squads to silence his son from giving testimony regarding Quesada's death merchants. Now themselves witnesses to Quesada's terrorism, Rivera and family are pursued by death squads. Aided by attorney David Holt, until he is murdered, and reporter Floyd Jefferson, who manages to bring the help of Able Team. *Justice by Fire*

Robbins, Dave—CIA rookie agent, killed by Armenian terrorists Ismet Kemal and Mustafa Izmir in CIA ambush. *Day of Mourning*

Robinson, Sandy—Charlie Green's secretary at WorldFiCor. Captured by Puerto Rican Nationals in takeover of tower. Rescued by Green and Able Team. *Tower of Terror*

Rojas, Sergeant—ruling police authority for district surrounding Santa Rosario del Norte. Allied with terrorist Luis Alsado in U.S. hostage plot. Posing as aid in Phoenix Force's investigation, leads Gary Manning into ambush. Killed by Manning. *Argentine Deadline*

Rojo—a.k.a. El Rojo, Availa Monroe's "loving" brother and leader of revolution to assassinate president of Mexico, he is funded and supported by Tate Monroe. Killed in Grimaldi air strike of Texas Irregulars hardsite. *Texas Showdown*

Rose, April—former primary mission controller and overseer of Stony Man Farm. This lady was Mack Bolan's closest ally since the final days of the Mafia campaigns. Killed in *Day of Mourning*.

Rosky, Col. Charles—U.S. Army captain in Vietnam, known as Can-Do Charlie. Retired out after acquittal in court-martial over a "little My Lai" in Trah Ninh province. Led Warco paramilitary forces. A Bolan kill. *Paramilitary Plot*

Roybal, Ricardo—a.k.a. **Rikki the Hyena**, mercenary killer for the new international Mafia don, Frank Contadina. A Bolan kill. *Terrorist Summit*

Ruiz, Fernando—"youth counselor" at L.A. Youth Action Corporation, the front organization for the DGI. Recruits killer punks and serves as lieutenant for Mario Silva. Betrays secret plans and escapes Silva's death squad, but is captured and interrogated by LAPD. *Army of Devils*

Running, Hans—captain of tanker *Contessa* captured by Lutfi. Saved from firing squad by Bolan and becomes Bolan's comrade in battle to regain the ship. Wounded. *Crude Kill*

Ryan, Paul—intelligence liaison officer, CIA, American Embassy, Japan. *Invisible Assassins*

Sadek, Salah Abul—Egyptian secret-police officer and liaison to CIA operations in Cairo. Leader of National Liberation Front Muslim terrorist organization. Killed by SAM-7 heat-seeking antiaircraft missile launched by Katzenelenbogen using Sadek's own terrorist network. *Cairo Countdown*

Salerno, Emilia—Red Justice Column terrorist and "heartless bitch" assigned to guard Louise DiAlto and daughter. A Bolan kill. *Tuscany Terror*

Samata Mako—martial-arts champion kidnapped by Zwilling Horde. Rescued by Bolan. *Bloodsport*

Santos, Raoul—a.k.a. The Butcher, does Leonard Jericho's dirty work. Skinned Eve Aguilar and earns a Bolan vengeance kill. *Libya Connection*

Samuels, Oliver—admiral, Office of Naval Intelligence, representative at top-secret conference of American and Japanese military-intelligence officers. Killed by Red Cell terrorists. *Dragon's Kill*

Sarafid, Emida—Yamani's second-in-command of Red Anvil's assault on Red Bluff Arsenal. Killed by Keio Ohara. *Atlantic Scramble*

Savasta, Gaspare Cesare—Italian senator with Communist affiliations and logistic ties to the Red Justice Column. Left by Bolan as "marked man" with the Column, Savasta escapes and turns informer. *Tuscany Terror*

Sazerac, Sweetie-Pie—French munitions supplier in Rio de Janeiro and professional consultant specializing in terrorist protection. Phoenix Force ally in the rescue of U.S. hostages held by Paraguayan terrorists. *Guerilla Games*

Scarr, Brendan—merc in South Africa during Simba Revolt, deserted post to rob nearby bank of diamonds and unknown valuable documents. Released from prison via deal with KGB to lead Soviets to cache. Bitten by Gabon viper, mercy killed by Katzenelenbogen. *Ambush on Blood River*

Schroder, Otto—ODESSA agent, Kortze's second-in-command. Killed by Keio Ohara in daylight attack on Katzenelenbogen and Ohara by ODESSA agents. *Ultimate Terror*

Schwarz, Hermann—Code-named Gadgets for his wizardry with electronic devices, this Vietnam vet has a genius-level IQ. Expert in explosives, quiet kills, guerilla tactics, a technological Apache. A hero of Able Team.

Seki Setsuko "Suki"—agent for Japan's internal-security service, poses as Commander Nakada's driver. Bolan ally in rescue and battle. *Invisible Assassins*

Severine, John—Soviet agent planted in U.S. Atomic Energy Program in 1950s. Organizer and head of the Outlaws' capture of Catalina Island to ransom nuclear sub for return to USSR. Posing as visitor, taken hostage along with islanders, detected and beaten. Rescued from islanders and returned to U.S. government by Able Team. *The Hostaged Island*

Shabaka, Abdul—born Leroi Jackson. Ex-Panther, ex-Death's Angel. Head of L.A. Youth Action Corporation's indoctrination and training center. Smuggled "crazy dust" for use on trained street punks to create Mario Silva's killer zombies. Captured by Flor Trujillo. *Army of Devils*

Shahkhia, Col. Ahmad—second-in-command to Khaddafi of Libyan army. Kremlin's choice for heir-apparent-puppet after coup. A Bolan kill. *Libya Connection*

al-Shawwa, Fuad—designer and engineer of Khatib's satellite-tracking system. Killed with Khatib in Bolan-Grimaldi air attack. *The New War*

Shepard, Ann—pregnant wife of Glenn Shepard the resistance organizer, defending Catalina Island. *The Hostaged Island*

Shepard, Glenn—Catalina Island resident, organizes neighbors in resistance fighting against the motorcycle gang. Wounded severely in the takeover. *The Hostaged Island*

Shepherd, Sarah—an aide to the U.S. Undersecretary of State, she is among the planeload of hostages taken by Paradine. *Paradine's Gauntlet*

Shinoda, Kenji—cryptographer, programmer and developer of controlled bacteria protein-based biochips. Sells out to Red Sun Chemical Corporation. Eliminated by Yamazaki *ninja*. *Invisible Assassins*

Shortner, Larry—head of VVAA—Vietnam Veterans for Affirmative Action. Kidnapped by Etalo Yareem, coerced to front for Anna Charissa's kidnap-ransom plot. Aides Bolan as diversion in final conflict. Kneecapped before being rescued by Bolan. Assigned with Latchford to Presidential Committee to the aid and readjustment of Viet vets. *Vulture's Vengeance*

Shroeder—member of Baader-Meinhof gang, hiding in France. Provides information for Red Brigades. *Paradine's Gauntlet*

Shyein, Saeb—Al-Fatah terrorist, liaison between Hydra heads Yoshida and Munoz. Captured in L.A. firefight, "questioned" by Lyons for information. *Stony Man Doctrine*

Silva, Mario—wealthy entrepreneur, founder and chairman of Los Angeles Youth Action Corporation, a front organization for the DGI—Dirección General de Inteligenciá—longtime Communist

Cuba agent, financed to further Cuba's interests in the U.S. However, Silva uses the funds to finance drug terrorism. Captured by LAPD while attempting to flee. *Army of Devils*

Silveres, Lieutenant—Brazilian officer captured by slavers and rescued by Able Team. Allies with Able Team and leads Xavante indians in assault of Wei Ho's City of Death. *Amazon Slaughter*

Simms, Geoffrey—company commander SAS. Formerly McCarter's CO and responsible for McCarter's applying for unknown assignment that led to his selection for Phoenix Force. Contact go-between for Stony Man Farm and McCarter when communications system fails. *The Fury Bombs*

Sioung Tham—tribal leader of the Meo guerillas and Army for the Restoration of National Independence. Former comrade of Bolan from Vietnam War, reallied in rescuing Colonel McFee. *Return to Vietnam*

Smalley, Roger—assistant police commissioner, heads conspiracy to protect Courtney Gilman for political gains. Killed by homicide detective Fawcett. *The Violent Streets*

Sommer, Wade—special investigator for Justice Department, liaison to Phoenix Force in *ninja* terrorist attacks against U.S. nuclear-power plants. Killed by a booby trap at Tigers of Justice headquarters. *Tigers of Justice*

Spinney—financial base for Khatib al-Suleiman's attack on the Panama Canal. Accidentally killed in an ambush when Bolan tries to capture him for interrogation. *The New War*

Stephens, Bad Louie—Cur to Big Jim Lane. A Bolan kill. *Island Deathtrap*

Stevens, Lou—elderly L.A. resident, attacked by Silva's punk killers. Defending his life and family, Stevens kills all five punks. Labeled a fascist vigilante butcher by Silva's LAYAC attorneys and served with wrongful-death suit. *Army of Devils*

Stevens, Max—captured Catalina Island resident, becomes organizer of resistance tactics by hostages. *The Hostaged Island*

Stiles, Bud—Kenlandsport fisherman forced by fear for his family into service for big Jim Lane. Murdered by Wilmer Moore for lobsterbed rights. *Island Deathtrap*

Stonewall—slimy second-in-command of Outlaws motorcycle gang. Executed by island resistance fighter Glen Shepard. *The Hostaged Island*

Strohman, Larry "The Bleeder"—J.D. Dante's soldier, spared by Bolan in return for information leading to Dante. *Flesh Wounds*

al-Suleiman, Khatib—Palestinian terrorist, found PLO too conservative. Leader of Colombian-based Hawks of the Revolution organized to pirate data from satellites to chart ship movements in Panama Canal. Their aim was to disrupt or destroy the flow of traffic through the canal. Killed by Bolan and Grimaldi. *The New War*

Swaine, Rory—Irish National Liberation Army soldier. Assumed killed. *White Hell*

Tado—chief of security for Hoshiro Company, the Japanese Red Cell headquarters. Former sumo wrestler, killed in hand-to-hand combat by Manning in Phoenix Force probe of Red Cell headquarters. *Dragon's Kill*

Takim, Sirhan—Turkish colonel and head of Paradine-guided army, the Turkish People's Liberation Army. Takim is delegated to lead the forces in revolution and to be installed as new ruler of Turkey. Bolan defeats Takim in an ambush and Paradine sends out a death squad for Bolan. Defeated again, Takim takes Kabrina hostage. In Bolan's raid and rescue, Takim is killed. *Double Crossfire*

Tanaga Zeko—infamous Japanese terrorist leader free-lancing with the Circle of the Red Sun. A Bolan kill atop a bullet train. *Invisible Assassins*

Thanh Le Van—commander of New York sect of People's Army of Vietnam. Leads Able Team into ambush at headquarters. Wounded by Lyons, Thanh is saved for interrogation. *Tower of Terror*

Thatcher, Gen. Arnold L.—chief of security, U.S. Army's nuclear, chemical and biological storage depot. Dying of cancer, he makes deal to sell Strain 7 to Lenny Jericho. Commits suicide when captured. *Libya Connection*

Toolan, Sean—head of Irish National Liberation Army. Killed by Phoenix Force and left suspended by a winch hook through his jaw. *White Hell*

Toppacardi, Danny "Tops"—leader of Mafia hit team working for Roger Smalley. Abducts Fran Traynor and Toni Blancanales. Killed by Rosario Blancanales. *The Violent Streets*

Torres, Julio—squad leader for Puerto Rican Nationals in takeover of WorldFiCor tower. Killed by Gadgets Schwarz. *Tower of Terror*

Towers, Bill—detective with LAPD and former partner of Carl Lyons. *Army of Devils, Stony Man Doctrine*

Tran Le—daughter of Meo tribal leader, Sioung Tham. Comrade-in-arms in Robert McFee's rescue from Viet military prison. *Return to Vietnam*

Traynor, Fran—in charge of Minneapolis rape crisis center, which aids Toni Blancanales. Abducted by Toppacardi and rescued by Bolan and Rosario Blancanales. *The Violent Streets*

Tresa, Samuel "Sammy the Shoe"—rare survivor of the Bolan war against the Mafia. Not so lucky when he is sent by Paradine to "hit" Marko Adamian. Bolan kill. *Double Crossfire*

Trujillo, Flor—agent from Drug Enforcement Agency. Detached to Stony Man as interface operative to handle drug and terrorism operations. Paramour of Carl Lyons. Shot down in helicopter chasing Abdul Shabaka's shipment of "crazy dust." *Stony Man Doctrine, Texas Showdown, Army of Devils*

Tuholske—medium-ranking KGB agent in Soviet embassy, Washington. Defected secretly to pass information to U.S. *Renegade Agent*

Turrin, Leo—Mob elder statesman (Leo "The Pussy" Turrin), undercover agent for Justice's Orgcrime Division, Washington lobbyist with connections, now officer of the Phoenix operation.

Unomundo—a.k.a. Klaust de la Unomundo-Stiglitz, a.k.a. Miguel de la Unomundo, Guatemalan drug billionaire, son of a self-exiled Nazi SS officer. Leader of profascist movement, the International Alliance, which aims to take over South American countries and establish a Nazi state. *Warlord of Azatlan*

Vallone, Gia—NOCS agent, infiltrates the Red Justice Column. Rescued by Bolan from safehouse torture room when cover is blown. Joins Bolan in search for kidnapped DiAltos. *Tuscany Terror*

Vang Ky—tribal headman and major in the CIA Montagnard army. Ally of Bolan against Tiger Enterprises. *Tiger War*

Vianke, Captain—NOCS control officer, Bolan's contact in RJC's DiAlto kidnapping. Also a paid contact of the Red Justice Column. Has Vallone, DiAlto and Bolan set up for ambush in NOCS headquarters. Killed by DiAlto. *Tuscany Terror*

Vigoury—USSR-trained killer on loan to terrorist network to hit Bolan. A Bolan kill. *Brothers in Blood*

Vitalli, Lavinia—medical specialist and developer of Formula Hyperactivity (HA27) and a mind-control drug. A Bolan kill. *Mountain Rampage*

Wade, Captain—head of security for Stony Man Farm but sells out to terrorist leader Al Miller. In assault against the farm, Wade is wounded by Miller merc, Pete Kagor, but survives to make a final attempt on Mack Bolan, killing April Rose instead. A Bolan kill. *Day of Mourning*

Ward, Thurston—ultraright mcgamillionaire committed to "salvation" of American prestige by paramilitary action vs. foreign "enemies." Founder and president of Warco conglomerate. A Bolan kill. *Paramilitary Plot*

Warner, Ed—Kenlandsport fisherman seeking help from Stony Man headquarters in fighting Big Jim Lane. Killed by Lane's goons. *Island Deathtrap*

Webster, Jack—Catalina Island teen captured by Outlaws motorcycle gang and forced to spy for resistance among townspeople held hostage. Flees during final assault by Able Team in rescue of hostages. *The Hostaged Island*

Wei Ho—ruthless head of the Wei clan and Chinese warlord of drugs and prostitution. A former mentor of China's Gang of Four, now plotting nuclear terrorism from South American fortress. Killed by Carl Lyons. *Amazon Slaughter*

Weng Shi—Lui's second-in-command of Tiger army. *Tiger War*

Werner, Klaus—Baader-Meinhof terrorist, killed by McCarter in raid of NATO missile site. *Ultimate Terror*

Whitecliff-Jones, Spencer—brains and organizer of Lutfi's terrorism scheme. A Bolan kill. *Crude Kill*

Wienberg, Solomon—has-been Nazi hunter and former ally of Katzenelenbogen from his days in the Mossad. *Ultimate Terror*

Wilkins, Simon—banker and member of American Economic Study Group in Argentina, taken hostage by Luis Alsado's terrorists. Rescued by Phoenix Force. *Argentine Deadline*

Williams, Josh—deed rancher at the Rocking JW. Bolan frees Josh and granddaughter from Kurt Holbein's goons. Aids Bolan in final escape from Paradise Valley. *Mountain Rampage*

Williams, Sara—granddaughter of Josh Williams, freed from Holbein's goon squad by Bolan. She becomes Bolan's ally in the destruction of the Paradise Valley hardsite. *Mountain Rampage*

Willoughby, Ray—senior Intercontinental Systems Ltd., hostage, killed by Chama during the Paraguayan army's raid on the terrorists. *Guerilla Games*

Wolfe, Richard—former small timer with connections to Augie Marinello, old activist associate of Luke Harker's, hiding out in Algeria doing "free-lance terrorism" for terrorist organizations. Wolfe is Harker's controlling force and the brains behind the bloodlust Third World People's Liberation Army. Mortally wounded by Mafia Black Ace Jon Carter and again by a soldier from his own ranks, Wolfe supplies Bolan with leads to Carter and Contadina before becoming a Bolan mercy kill. *Terrorist Summit*

Wynn, Janet—niece of Phoenix Force's Rafael Encizo. Baited into heroin addiction by Tiger Enterprises, she is also killed by their assassins. *Tiger War*

Xavante, Thomas Jefferson—Xavante Indian guide, ally and combat leader in Able Team's assault on Wei Ho's City of Death. *Amazon Slaughter*

Y Bo—Meo warrior allied with Bolan in Colonel McFee's rescue. *Return to Vietnam*

Yagoda, Col. Boris—KGB agent dealing with Brendan Scarr in going after cache of diamonds. Falls to death during hand-to-hand combat with Bolan. *Ambush on Blood River*

Yamani, Janda—a.k.a. First Lieutenant Ramos, Colonel Ballard's adjutant at Red Bluff Arsenal. Jeddah terrorist working as sleeper agent within the military ranks to set up takeover of arsenal and transportation for stolen Dessler Laser Submachine Guns. Killed by Rafael Encizo. *Atlantic Scramble*

Yamazaki Hideo—self-professed Lord of the Red Sun, mob overlord of the Circle of the Red Sun. Left dying by Bolan from wounds and chemical death, commits hara-kiri. *Invisible Assassins*

Yareem, Etalo—terrorist, revolutionary and leader of guerilla band in badlands of Nicaragua. Working on his own hoping to attract the attention and support of Cuba. Arranges the kidnapping of diplomat figure Anna Charissa and demands ransom and U.S. withdrawal from Latin America. Fills his merc ranks via his recruiting operation, the Vietnam Veterans for Affirmative Action, or merely by kidnapping. A Bolan kill. *Vulture's Vengeance*

Yazid, Karim—head of Khomeini's assassination team sent to kill former SAVAK member, General Nazarour. A Bolan kill. *Iranian Hit*

Yoichi, Prof. Ouzu—organizer of Japanese Red Cell with KGB and North Korean UNGII backing. Created EES-electroencephalo stimulator for interpreting brain waves for interrogation. Killed by Katzenelenbogen in assault of Edward Oshimi's castle. *Dragon's Kill*

York, Byron—onetime SDS activist, former Weather Underground radical and former fiancé of April Rose. The leader of a group of fanatical survivalists, York—still wanted for crimes committed with the Weatherman—is forced to aid Weatherman J.D. Dante, April and Bolan "enlist" York as a guide out of his survival camp and to Dante on the Radical Express. York is killed by his own survivalist zealots escaping the camp. *Flesh Wounds*

Yoshida Kinosuke—leader of Japan's United Red Army and responsible for assembling Hydra's army of terrorists. With Hydra's failure imminent, Yoshida dons the uniform of the *ninja* and kills co-Hydra head Fedorenko. Yoshida is killed by Bolan in a final battle on Hydra's island base. *Stony Man Doctrine*

Yoto Shikimi—sensei at Zembu Dojo martial-arts school, a second-level terrorist base for the Japanese Red Cell. Killed by Katzenelenbogen in Phoenix Force probe of Hoshiro Company. *Dragon's Kill*

Zaki—Egyptian "taximan" and battle ally with Able Team against Muslim Brotherhood. *Cairo Countdown*

Zeigler, Gen. Adolf—former Nazi officer in exile, now head of ODESSA's Intelligence Operations. He carries the scars of a previous encounter with Yakov Katzenelenbogen when the latter was in the Mossad. Orders a hit on Katz, which fails. *Ultimate Terror*

Ziemba—Nabu tribesman seeking vengeance for the murder of his brother by General Mumungo's Leopard Patrol. Allies with Bolan to hunt down Mumungo's forces. *Ambush on Blood River*

Zossimov, Fyodor—"technical director" from Moscow's international terrorism desk, conspiring with Weather Underground leader J.D. Dante in a terrorist plot to spray napalm rain over OPON Festival. Zossimov is a Bolan kill with the napalm rain. *Flesh Wounds*

Zuniga, Anthony—leader of the Puerto Rican Nationals in the terrorist takeover of World Financial Corporation. Zuniga and his vanguard are killed in an Able Team assault of the tower. *Tower of Terror*

The Terrorist Organizations

from

Mack Bolan #39–#62
Able Team #1–#9
Phoenix Force #1–#9
Stony Man Doctrine

Bolan's war is as old as mankind, and I make this point in The Executioner #39: *The New War*, whose title indicates only a new enemy, a new dramatic direction. Actually, the Mafia is not nearly as strong now as when Bolan first began his one-man vigilante war; but I would have reshaped the series even if this was not true because I believe that the hard challenge of today is not organized crime, but the organized savagery that we see today as international terrorism. These people, the terrorists, are the new wolf packs threatening the forward progress of the human procession. They are a plague running wild in the world that threatens to wipe out everything civilized man has achieved after centuries of agonizing struggle against the forces of mindless brutality. As the greatest threat to the free world, they are therefore the greatest threat to Bolan's world. For realism if for nothing else, I *had* to send Bolan into this "new" war.

—Don Pendleton

Al-Fatah—Palestinian terrorist organization. *Stony Man Doctrine*

Anzen Sekai—pacifist antinuclear organization front for the Tigers of Justice. *Tigers of Justice*

Army of the People's Republic of Ireland a.k.a. Irish Raiders—creation of Irish Socialist Republican Army dissident Seamus Riley. *The Fury Bombs*

Baader-Meinhof—*Ultimate Terror*

Black Cobras—personal army of Gen. Jeremiah Blackwell. *Aswan Hellbox*

Circle of the Red Sun—mutation of the Jonin, Yakuza and personal power structure of Hideo Yamazaki. *Invisible Assassins*

Democratic Liberation Front—faction fighting Unomundo. *Kill School*

Dirección General de Inteligencia—DGI—*Stony Man Doctrine, Army of Devils*

El Ejercito de los Guerreras Blancos—Salvadoran death squad linked to Unomundo. *Justice by Fire*

Ejercito Revolucionario del Pueblo—ERP—*Argentine Deadline*

Eritrean People's Liberation Front—cohorts of General Blackwell in Aswan Dam plot. *Aswan Hellbox*

FALN—*Tower of Terror*

Grey Dog—splinter faction of the IRA and INLA. *White Hell*

Hawks of the Revolution—PLO-inspired organization of terrorist Khatib al-Suleiman. *The New War*

Hydra—conglomerate organization of KGB, DGI and United Red Army of Japan. *Stony Man Doctrine*

International Alliance—union of Central American groups to create a single state under Unomundo. *Warlord of Azatlan, Kill School*

Irish National Liberation Army—dissident arm of the Irish Republican Army. *White Hell*

Irish Raiders—see Army of the People's Republic of Ireland

Irish Republican Army—IRA—*The Fury Bombs*

Irish Socialist Republican Army—ISRA—see Army of the People's Republic of Ireland

Japanese Red Cell—terrorist creation of Prof. Edward Oshimi. *Dragon's Kill*

Jeddah—*Atlantic Scramble*

Justice Commandos of Armenian Genocide—*Day of Mourning*

Khmer Rouge—*Amazon Slaughter*

Leopard Patrol—Kurandan General Mumungo's personal army. *Ambush on Blood River*

Los Angeles Youth Action Corporation—Cuban agent Mario Silva's front organization for the Dirección General de Inteligencia. *Army of Devils*

Muslim Brotherhood—*Cairo Countdown*

National Liberation Front—*Cairo Countdown*

Odessa—*Ultimate Terror*

Organizacion Democratica Nacionalista—ORDEN—*Justice by Fire*

Outlaws—Motorcycle gang with Soviet guidance. *The Hostaged Island*

Palestinian People's Army—*Sold for Slaughter*

People's Army of Vietnam—*Tower of Terror*

Popular Liberation Forces—*Kill School*

Provisional Irish Republican Army—PROVOS—*The Fury Bombs*

Puerto Rican Nationals—terrorists devoted to the freedom of Puerto Rico and the release of Puerto Ricans from U.S. prisons. *Tower of Terror*

Red Anvil—Libyan terrorist organization, splinter of Jeddah headed by Khader Ghazawi. *Atlantic Scramble*

Red Brigade—best-known member of the Italian terrorist coalition known as the Organization. *Renegade Agent, Crude Kill, Paradine's Gauntlet*

Red Justice Column—organization of hard-core felons recruited as liberation fighters. *Tuscany Terror*

Secret Liberation Army of Armenia—SALA—mercenary army purchased by Marko Adamian and World Armenian Congress. *Double Crossfire*

Staats-Sicherheits-Dienst—SSD—*Ultimate Terror*

Texas Irregulars—mercenary army purchased by Tate Monroe to assassinate the president of Mexico and join forces with Mexican troops in revolution. *Texas Showdown*

Third World People's Liberation Army—private terrorist army for hire to any paying party. Created by an alliance of terrorist groups. *Terrorist Summit*

Tiger Enterprises—private terror corporation created by drug warlord Liu Hsaio. *Tiger War*

Tigers of Justice—Japanese union of victims, relatives and descendants of the nuclear war in Japan bent on retribution by the destruction of U.S. nuclear facilities. *Tigers of Justice*

Turkish People's Liberation Army—Turkish terrorist army guided by KGB contract worker Paradine plotting a heroin flood as an assault against the U.S. and as financing for overthrow of Turkish government. *Double Crossfire*

Unione Corse—Corsican syndicate. *Paradine's Gauntlet*

United Red Army—third head of Hydra, represented by Kinosuke Yoshida. *Stony Man Doctrine*

Universal Devotees—an Eastern-oriented religious cult founded by Nguyen Van Minh. *Doomsday Disciples*

Vietnam Veterans for Affirmative Action—a front for a mercenary-recruitment operation for Etalo Yareem's guerilla band. *Vulture's Vengeance*

Warco—chemical corporation headed by Thurston Ward dedicated to paramilitary power over negotiated power. *Paramilitary Plot*

Weather Underground—an old radical group by modern terrorism standards, reaping fresh blood by a new alliance with Moscow's terrorism think tanks. Led by Weatherman J.D. Dante and backed by Soviet Death Deliveryman Fyodor Zossimov. *Flesh Wounds*

World Armenian Congress—terrorist organization in the making, serving as a fund raiser for the Armenian cause to purchase a fighting force. *Double Crossfire*

Yakuza—*Invisible Assassins*

Zwilling Horde—politically and philosophically aligned with Black Sunday, the Zwilling Horde specializes in torture. A small organization forced to rob and ransom for its keep and embittered by the big backing of its terrorist brothers. *Bloodsport*

Dear Don

Dear Don:

I am presently serving with the U.S. Army at Fort Benning, Georgia. I have read and relished every one of the Mack Bolan series, and anxiously await each new book. I devour Able Team and Phoenix Force.

My basic question is, why isn't Mack Bolan on the silver screen? If it is for lack of the actor to play Bolan, I feel that I could fit the bill. I am six foot three and weigh approximately 208 pounds.

I am familiar with weapons and I understand the Bolan personality. I strongly feel I could fill Bolan's shoes.

Bolan is a military man and I understand the military concept and Mack's basic love for human life. I understand why he is who he is. Within him there is a part of every man and woman who are honest citizens.

Bolan is a solitary soul who believes that life is sacred and that everything must be done to protect the innocents. I really like the development in *Island Deathtrap*, where Bolan sees the weak links in the system. As you have written, Bolan has to be a person "untainted" by others.

I have a particular kinship to Bolan, and I would like to be given the opportunity to prove this. You have written books about an ideal that is as old as man's love for freedom. I feel that love, and I offer my help to put it on the screen. I now give a small portion of this by serving my country. I will always "stay hard" because when a person gives in to the monsters, he allows a portion of himself to be torn away.

—R.B., Georgia

Many, many readers have asked me about an Executioner movie, but I have to admit you're the first to offer your own services as the star. Well, good for you. I wish I could take you up on it, but the film rights to The Executioner have been held for some time now by Burt Reynolds (whose

interest is in the production side of the project only), and Gold Eagle is not expected to play any part in the casting. We do forward inquiries about the movie, however, so maybe you'll see the inside of a studio yet! I appreciate your words; you're a good soldier, and I share your eagerness to see a good Executioner movie one of these days.

Dear Don:

I hope these few lines find you well. Sir, I am currently serving a prison term in a correctional institution for a number of serious crimes. A hardcase. Yeah. Sure. Well, I had never heard of you or The Executioner until I came here. A guy had the entire Executioner series and at first I thought that Mack "The Bastard" Bolan was just another hardcase bent on bloody destruction.

But after I got into the series. . . . Sir, I began to see the man and not the execution. It is very difficult for me to put my feelings into words—hell, I can't exactly say what it is I feel. But it's a throbbing. From the core, the soul. Most fascinating.

In any event, I'm proud now to say that Mack Bolan has succeeded in making me feel so ashamed of myself that for a long time I felt like scum. He has made me completely reevaluate my values, morals. . . and heart. I'll never again participate in criminal activity. Thank you, Mr. Pendleton, and thank that guy. Mack is dynamite. Mack is a creation in calm fury against acts of cowardly viciousness and treason against mankind.

The universe has chosen its grim reaper, its appointed executioner. Destiny has whispered to Bolan, and he has come to look it in the face, and it is death. Ah, his soul is weary. That last mile is hell. The longest mile of his life. And yet he comes through like a champion. Man, that guy must have a lot of love in that big heart of his. I'm going to walk that mile to the line with him.

"Everything in the universe matters," as the guy once said to himself. Yeah, it sure does. I've pulled myself up from the muck now, thanks to Mack. I salute you, sir.

—R.F., Ohio

Thanks, my friend, on behalf of Mack. I'm delighted to hear of your progress on the good path. For many, Mack's route through the savage pastures of war everlasting is in one aspect at least—the pain and suffering—not so very different from their own mired passage through the jungle of life. Mack cares, as you point out. And that's what counts, that's what makes all the difference in the world. Welcome to our legion of Bolan/Able Team/Phoenix Force fans. We have all kinds of folks who enjoy the adventures we're producing. Servicemen and law-enforcement people, of course. A surprising number of female readers, a lot of very young ones (Able Team has become a cult among teenagers), and a respectable representation from the various professions—in fact the *New York Daily News* saw fit to report recently that a man in a pin-striped suit had been sighted reading *Stony Man Doctrine* on the subway! To my personal knowledge the range of readers is from a nine-year-old boy to a ninety-four-year-old retired Army officer, so you're in good company, pal, and it's where you belong.

Dear Don:

My friend and I have been talking about an idea for one of your books. What about making a special book giving information about Stony Man Farm? Things like its blueprint and other items, so we could get a better idea of what the farm looks like and how it works.

Also, what about giving detailed descriptions on weapons like you did in *Tuscany Terror*?

I have one more idea. What about giving a list of all the characters in the Stony Man stories?

If you and your team of writers would think about doing this, I and my friends would sure appreciate it because we are very loyal readers.

—S.M., California

You got it!

Dear Don:

Writing a fan letter is an unusual thing for me to do. I consider it an imposition on a busy author, and it is probably just ego talking anyway, but I felt impelled to write this one.

I am a Mack Bolan addict—not fan, but addict—and nobody is more surprised about it than I am! I doubt that I am your average reader. I am thirty-nine, a housewife but not a very conventional one. I founded with my husband the organization mentioned in the letterhead, have run it and published its magazine for the last fourteen years. We have four children and dozens of animals. I am a voracious and very eclectic reader of fiction and nonfiction—and here I am a Mack Bolan nut! How in the heck did it happen?

I first read of the Executioner in that handy little compendium of mystery, *Murder Ink*. I am a great fan of mystery novels, but of the English kind with tea parties and vicars, not machine guns! However, I had gotten hooked on Travis McGee, and *Murder Ink*. rated The Executioner second to him and gave it an "A" for Sincerity and Originality, two of my favorite traits. We have a secondhand bookstore nearby, so it didn't cost me much of anything to try one, though it has cost me a good deal since! I started with "I'll read one or two," progressed to "I'll read the ones I haven't read and pass them along" (I've sent a good many to my son in the Army), and finally ended up with the collector's fanatic gleam in my eye and book catalogs from your publisher! I now have every single one (with the ones I couldn't find on order) and am hungrily waiting for the next.

What the HELL happened to me? I guess I suddenly realized that this is *the* Good against Evil story—and the Good is WINNING! You get hooked, at least I did.

And I am hooked on Mack himself and somehow on his particular adventures and something in your own writing that I cannot describe, but you really mean what you say and say it extremely well!

Well there we are, a fan letter. The last one I wrote, out of all the thousands of authors I have read, was to Guy Murchie for *Song of the Sky* when I was fourteen. This is probably my last one—but thank you, I so enjoy real treasure.

—B.H., Texas

Thanks a million for your letter. I believe that Mack Bolan's appeal is due in large measure to the fact that he is a human being in perfect balance: compassionate and warmly human yet possessed of an iron will that enables him to effectively champion the causes he feels so deeply. My women readers relate to him, I think, not just because Bolan represents the idealized man but because heroism and selfless dedication to ideals is as much a feminine as a masculine trait. One of my female fans once remarked that Bolan is a father-mother figure. On reflection, I was inclined to agree. The masculine form of aggressive behavior is typified by conquest and idealized combat, while feminine aggressiveness is more often related to the practical needs of home and family. Though Bolan is moved by ideals, he is also motivated by the more protective mechanisms.

Dear Don:
I have just finished reading the second greatest book I have ever read: *Stony Man Doctrine*. I am proud to say this book moved me to tears, from the very first words to the very last. I will no doubt reread this magnificent book over and over again.

I have read every Mack Bolan story, every Able Team story and every Phoenix Force story. I must say I feel a little closer to Mack, Gadgets and Rosario Blancanales because I, too, am a veteran of the Vietnam conflict. I believe these men would know where I'm coming from and where I'm trying to go.

God of earth and universe bless you, Mr. Pendleton. Your writing has touched a part of me I thought had died over there.

Stony Man Doctrine made me see that there are some who still care and are willing to fight and even die so others can know the same.

Keep on writing, guys. If your words can move a bitter, uncaring person like me, I know they will move others.

—J.K., Florida

Perhaps because the three Stony Man weapons known as Bolan, Able Team and Phoenix Force are all in it, *Stony Man Doctrine* is clearly a milestone in action-adventure history. I can say this with all modesty, for the acknowledgment page of *Stony Man Doctrine* tells the story—the talent that glows within the book is Dick Stivers. It was Dick who foresaw a real world in which Cuban nationals would be exhorted by Castro to kill Americans on sight. We were all way ahead of our time in that book—I say so with grief—but I know it will stand in years far beyond its own time as a beacon of what can be achieved in this kind of literature. But wait a minute, I'm saying all this before the world has had a chance to read the *next* Super Bolan! It's called *Terminal Velocity*, and it's a 384-page blockbuster introducing Bolan's loneliest war. Available soon.

Dear Don:

I have recently completed your novel *Stony Man Doctrine*, and as is usual with your books, I enjoyed it. I have always admired your action scenes and your attention to detail.

I was therefore disappointed in your references to the U.S. Coast Guard. Vessels of the Coast Guard are designated USCGC (C for Cutters, from the historic Revenue Cutter Service), not USS as in your chapter 25. Also the deck guns on cutters are either 3″ or 5″, not 4″.

As a member of the United States' oldest continuous service, I felt bound to point out these discrepancies to ensure nonrepetition. Again, I thank you for providing great entertainment, which certainly helps pass time at sea.

—B.G., Virginia

Rest assured the errors will not be repeated. One of them was a misprint, one a mistake; I'll leave you to guess which was which. It is a privilege to be corrected by a serviceman such as yourself, and I take my hat off to the U.S. Coast Guard, a tremendous group of men and a fine fleet of cutters.

Dear Don:

I'm only a kid, but a kid who has read and enjoyed every one of Mack Bolan's adventures, from *War Against the Mafia* through *Brothers in Blood*. I loved them and I'm eagerly waiting for more.

Mack Bolan, a.k.a. John Phoenix, rather resembles my brother. Both accept the oncomings of life and live through them. Both know that death and the losing of loved ones is a large fact of living, even though it's hard to withstand the tremendous impact of death's fist.

When I first heard of Bolan, and how much he resembles my big bro, I had to read your books. Holy cow, was I ever surprised at your ideas! I can still remember how I felt after finishing *War Against the Mafia*. I said to myself, "now here's a real tough guy. A kind of man who stands for the American way. Bolan is the ideal American man." My emotions were all mixed up. I didn't know what to feel, sad for his parents and sister Cindy, happy because he stood up for what he believed in, or angered at finding out how real the Mafia is in realistic terms.

Right now I'm sitting at my family's picnic table with the sun glowing brilliantly on a great day. I have just finished reading *Brothers in Blood* and I thought it was. . .it was. . .heck! There are no words to describe how great I thought it was!

I was thrilled out of my cornwackers with the remembrance of Mack's strong-hearted younger brother Johnny and the mention of Val. Oh yeah, Valentina Querente, what a gal!

Well, I've taken up enough of your time. Thanks for being you and giving me hours and hours of pleasurable reading time.

—S.L., Michigan

You're not taking up my time, kid. I'm glad you liked *Brothers in Blood*. You're not the only one, you know. That's a really popular book. It's also the first to introduce, through the Vigoury connection, the domino attack sequence devised by the Department of Terror that has brought Bolan to his present pass.

Dear Don:
My husband and I have just finished reading Able Team #2, *The Hostaged Island*. We are both fans of the Executioner series and are glad to see the new Able Team and Phoenix Force added.

There was one thing that upset us this time. You see, my husband is presently a sergeant in the U.S. Army. He is also an auto mechanic, Vietnam veteran and a biker.

I am a wife, mother, computer operator and a biker.

Bikers are people. Not weird psychopathic killers. As bikers we do not approve of the way you present "bikers" in this story.

Your stories are always very fast-action and exciting. For the most part they are very accurate in detail.

I hope you really hear what I'm trying to say. Bikers just wan
to be left alone. They want to ride free in the wind. They, lik
Mack Bolan, are not out to look for violence. But they do no
turn their backs if people mess with them.

I had better stop now before this gets any longer. Thank yo
for all the years of entertainment. We wish you success in th
future. Just go light on bikers, huh? We've had enough bac
press.

—G.M., Florid

**You're absolutely right, of course. One percent or less of th
motorcycling world can be classed as troublemakers, an
that's a damn sight smaller percentage than you'll find i
most groups. May you ride free in the wind for as long a
Mack flies free! Our point in *The Hostaged Island* was that
bike gang had sold out to the KGB—and *that's* when you ge
into trouble, real trouble if the grizzly fate of groups wh
have toyed with Moscow's terrorbrokers are anything to g
by. Just because you dig bikes and live "outside" of societ
and have to make do—like all of us—in difficult times
doesn't mean you have to sell out to the KGB, ever, and tha
was "Horse's" mistake. He paid for it as surely as do a
those other guys from other walks of life who come at Bola
from the wrong side of right and wrong. Stay hard, yo
two, and good reading!**

Dear Don:
I have just finished reading Able Team #8, *Army of Devils*.
was really upset that you killed off Flor Trujillo.

I thought it was great in *Stony Man Doctrine, Texas Show
down* and *Army of Devils* that Carl Lyons had met a woman wh
could become special, a girl of his own, someone he could b
completely open and natural with. He wouldn't have to worr
all the time about the life he had chosen because she was rig
there with him, fighting toward the same goals.

I even thought that maybe he would settle down and not be so wild. At the rate he's going, there's a possibility that someday he'll end up putting the team in danger of getting themselves killed.

Carl is made out of the same mold as Mack and is very much like him. Is there no place for any of these men to have a truly personal life of their own?

Flor had become a part of the team and knew exactly what she was doing and why. Her reasons were the same as those of any other member of the Stony Man team.

Haven't you opened the door for Carl to go crazy, become a truly wildassed warrior? I remember in Able Team #5, *Cairo Countdown*, Mack said he'd have to take Carl aside and talk with him about his actions.

I think Dick Stivers is great to be able to step in and take on the Able Team stories, so do keep them coming, and keep showing us how these men are living large and staying hard!

—D.M., Missouri

I'm proud of Dick's major effort with Able Team—there's genius in his ability to place you in the middle of combat. And that's exactly why I have to let him do what he has to in Able Team, even if it means depriving Carl of that beautiful and heroic figure, Flor Trujillo. There have been many other allies of Mack and his men who have fallen in combat. Holstrom, Ripper, Andrzej Konzaki and, of course, Eve Aguilar and April Rose.... It is a tragedy when the world loses characters so pure. How it burns! But remember— death is part of a process, a new perception, as Margerita said. One of my readers, C.H. of Missouri, puts it splendidly in a letter to me the other day: "If life were a maze you would never find the end, for the end is death, and death itself is a new beginning." By the way, I think Carl Lyons will do just fine, but keep reading—anything could happen in stories as realistic as ours.

Dear Don:

This is the absolute first fan letter I've ever written to anyone.
have all of Gar Wilson's Phoenix Force books up to #7. I love
them! I've read many of your Mack Bolan books and I under
stand you helped Gar start writing Phoenix Force. I think he
writes so much like you, yet with a style all his own!

Mack Bolan was my first great pleasure (besides girls), but
my endless fascination with David McCarter has surpassed
even good ol' Mack. Granted, I love the action, but wow
McCarter is my kind of guy!

Some young people like getting blown away on punk music
and drugs and stuff like that, but not me. I'll bask in the glory
every time Phoenix successfully completes another mission
The American foreign legion is doing a great job. Phoenix
Force forever!
                                                    —J.M., New York

**And you're doing a great job too! Gar's terrific—see the
Phoenix Force piece later in this book for a taste of some of
his wilder new stuff. But where would any of us writers be if
our readers did not take our writing seriously (as we our
selves do), and thus find it of benefit to their lives? Your
words are every bit as exciting to us, as the very best Gold
Eagle adventures are to you.**

Dear Don:

I've been reading your books for two years now. My mom and
dad read them too. We let each other read books from each
other's collections and when a book comes up missing, all hell
breaks loose like in *Stony Man Doctrine*.

When I was in the U.S. Army field artillery, I saw a guy get
discharged from the Army because his eye was off one degree
or something; another guy had the strength of four men but
couldn't extend his arm to where his elbow would lock, so he
was discharged too. A friend of mine has one arm shorter than

the other, but we used to knock the hell out of the preppies in high-school football. I have a slight limp, and I was the only person to place in varsity long-distance track.

Whoever decided to put Katz in Phoenix Force had a great idea. Katz shows people they should not judge others by what's on the outside, but by something that can never be changed, which is the inside. Katz is a job well done.

—M.R., Mississippi

I like you and I like your family. May the fur fly in your house for as long as we can put out the books!

Dear Don:
I have just finished reading Mack Bolan #39, *The New War*, for the second time. I'm even more excited than I was the first time I read it, when I was so excited that I could not really assimilate everything. I really love (and I don't know a better word to describe my feelings) the prologue. It says it all as far as Mack as a man and his philosophy of life are concerned, without being too heavy. I particularly like the words on responsibility to be found in the third paragraph of page 11. If only there really were a few large men such as Mack who could see the Four Horsemen of Fanaticism, Revolution, Terror, and Holocaust by Technology, and ride them to their deaths.

I have only one question, however. Sometimes when I'm reading, I find it hard to come to grips with the story unless the time factor is explained. One thing that has been nagging at the back of my mind since I started rereading the books is how many years has Mack waged his war of attrition? The picture on the cover of *The New War* shows a Mack Bolan a bit older and a little heavier than the pictures on the earlier books, and he doesn't look quite as dark as he used to. Or is that due to his role camouflage ability, or maybe plastic surgery?

And would it be possible to work some R&R into the books

so that Mack has a week of rest between assignments? remember when he left Detroit he spent a little time in green pastures with Toby Ranger, and I know you allowed him some time to rest and assimilate his new groups before he went in search of Laconia. Mack is a superior man, but he is still human, and doesn't he need some recreation once in a while?

—S.A., Florida

Bolan was created in the late 1960s, while the Vietnam war still raged. I developed a mature character with plenty of combat background, an Army "lifer" who could conceivably survive the sort of adventures I had in mind for him. In the time frame given for Bolan's military experience (from age eighteen to thirty, or twelve years), it was no stretch whatever to give him some background in the Korean conflict. By the mid-seventies I was beginning to receive puzzled notes from fans wondering how old Bolan must have been during the Korean conflict. One reader worked it out in his head that Bolan must have been about nine years old. But, of course, the "now time" of the series is considerably shorter than publication time, real-world time, since Bolan may blitz through an average adventure in a matter of days or even hours—much less than it took to produce the book relating that adventure. His war against the Mafia, even played out thirty-eight times, spanned no more than a couple of years.

I appreciate the fact that you'd like to see all the personal stuff of Bolan's life, including his time off, because you are interested in the character and want some simple human comfort to come to him. But I believe your interest exists just because this man is embattled, forever discomforted, forever poised between life and death.

Mack's features have indeed been changed by plastic surgery. You can see only half his face on the Vietnam War portrait that is the cover of this book. But he's not been changed *that* much. You can always recognize him by his eyes: icy and blue and something else. . . .

Dear Don:

I can't remember when I first started reading The Executioner, but it was a good while back.

I am twenty-four years old and have been in the U.S. Army (and still am) for the past five. Mack has seen myself and many friends through many, many tours of duty as Charge of Quarters or Sergeant of the Guard.

I'm also into art and Gil Cohen's covers are always excellent. I do have a question: is there any way an Executioner fan like myself could obtain an original? It would be a piece of artwork I'd treasure forever.

Please pass on my thanks to Gil for his painting; it seeds the imagination, and the text is like the blossoming of the seed.

—J.H., Maryland

I agree. Gil's art is great. It works exactly as you describe it. Occasionally Gil will have a piece of art up for sale at a convention, but its value is very considerable and is rising all the time. Why don't you write to Gil Cohen directly, c/o Gold Eagle Books, and tell him about yourself? Gil is a veteran of every single Bolan mision, and he has worked tirelessly and brilliantly to produce the best covers in the business. God bless him.

Dear Don:

I have been a reader of your books since I was in Vietnam. They helped prepare me for what I was to face the next day. Mack Bolan and I have something in common; we were both deep-penetration and termination specialists, except that Mack was in the Army and I was in the Marine Corps.

One big thing that got me to read your books is the personal tragedy that started Mack on his home-front war. Many Vietnam vets experienced misfortunes of the same grieviousness if not of the same magnitude. I myself am one. Due to my assignment in Vietnam being stamped Top Secret, I was not even accorded the dignity of having my Vietnam service listed in my official record. Despite being wounded, I was not awarded the Purple Heart or any other medal, because as far as the government was concerned, I was technically not in Vietnam but stationed somewhere else at the time. Because of what happened to me, sometimes I feel as though Mack and I are of the same blood.

Since I've been out of the service, I have served as a soldier of fortune for six years under a false name to protect my U.S. citizenship. I have fought Communists in Africa, Afghanistan, El Salvador and Nicaragua and can understand firsthand the threat Communists pose to our country and the free world. I was delighted when you came out with Mack and Able Team and Phoenix Force fighting this new and greater threat. They are men so real to me that I think of myself as one of them.

I've read every one of the Executioner series at least twice and I've read every Able Team and Phoenix Force book four times. I have been meaning to write you about these books for a long time, but it wasn't until recently that I've been able to face what I have been through and found the courage to write.

—G.M., Pennsylvania

Yours has been a rich but troubled life. You're finding more courage all the time. I think you're going to make it A-OK.

Dear Don:
I really like the new series. It has given me entertainment plus made me realize the actual problem the world has these days. A few people think your books are a little gung ho and too bloody,

out terrorism is real and wasn't intended to fill the people of the world with joy but to infest their hearts with fear.

Being in the Sixth Fleet, I realize the threat of hostile enemies is all around us. I really feel disgusted that it comes back to the Russians almost every time. Their culture may be okay, but the government is so paranoid about the U.S. and our allies that both open and secret forces are being built against us.

Our mission is to maintain the sea lanes. It's very important since eighty-eight percent of the U.S.A.'s goods comes from the oceans. I was already aware of the terrorist situation before I started reading your books. Now my mind feels somewhat at ease that someone is doing something. I wish that I was in Mack's place, or on his force.

I've been to many countries and feel fortunate to have done so, but it always comes down to this, that my country and freedom are to be cherished and protected as long as I'm able. I was in London, England, shortly after the IRA's attack on the Horse Guards, and the atmosphere in the city was tense and nervous as hell—as if something terrible could happen again at any moment. That's enough to ruin people's lives. I swear, Don, that sometimes I feel so bad for the people who lose their lives to senseless cold-blooded murder. I believe that terrorism should be stopped with the tactics that Striker uses and I respect your writings for doing just that.

Some people would not understand what I'm saying, so it feels good for me to say it to someone who does.

—D.B., New York

You're talking patriotism and you can bet that sounds good to me. I can measure your self-worth from the way your words stand tall. It takes on a special meaning for me to tell a guy like you to live large.

Finally, I've received a fascinating letter from my colleague, Gar Wilson, author of Phoenix Force. I'd like to

share it with you. Gar never fails to put my mind into the thick of the headlines!

Dear Don:

Once upon a time, only the rich and famous had to be concerned with kidnapping. Nowadays however, as you know, virtually anyone can be abducted by terrorist fanatics. Many people seem unaware of the danger. May I offer these words of advice to those whose freedom may be threatened at any time?

If you are held hostage by terrorists, try to keep a cool head. Easy to say, tough to do. Panic or hysteria won't help you under any circumstances. You *must control* your emotions in a crisis situation.

Never threaten or mock terrorist captors. Terrorists are emotionally unstable. They will almost certainly respond to verbal abuse with violence. However, do not mistake crazed extremism for stupidity. Most terrorists are intelligent and well-educated. Never underestimate them.

Never pretend to suddenly embrace the radical beliefs of your captors or claim you want to be friends with them. It's a natural—or at least typical—reaction, to identify with the aggressor in order to neutralize the impact of the threat, but it's a serious mistake. Terrorists are not interested in your friendship and only rarely are they duped by such a tactic. They are apt to consider it an insult to their intelligence. Hostages have been tortured to death by terrorists for this offense.

Conditions are different in situations of hostage holding over an extended period of time, especially when the terrorists have access to either a secluded area or are operating in a country with a ruling government that sympathizes with their cause. Under those circumstances, the captors may attempt to convert hostages to join their cause.

If you are being held in such a situation and your captors order you to salute an enemy flag or bow to the head savage then do it. To be starved, tortured or killed because you tried to play it tough is not courageous. If you are weak from hunger or injured from beatings, you will have less of a chance to escape or overpower a guard should an opportunity occur. Machismo is suicidal in such a situation.

The best thing to do is keep quiet and offer no resistance. Most terrorists do not intend to kill their hostages. One cannot use a corpse to bargain with.

Terrorists usually make no secret of the fact that they are holding hostages. Often where the captives are being held is public knowledge. Thus, there is an excellent chance that law-enforcement personnel will attempt to rescue you.

Stay alert. You may be able to help your rescuers if you see them before the terrorists do. A well-timed distraction— feigning a heart attack or pretending to break down in tears— might assist the rescue team. If you try it, do not overact. Terrorists are unstable and highly strung individuals. Hysterics might actually frighten them into using their weapons.

In summary: Try to stay calm, keep your mouth shut and be ready to duck. If you are *absolutely positive* that your captors are about to kill you, you have nothing to lose by making a desperate lunge for a terrorist's weapon—or his throat.

Roll Call
from Mack Bolan's journal

Hell, I'm no writer, but I've been there, I know how it is in Beirut. I know how it's been in the latest fractured months, the city crushed by dark and terrible tides, its war no less everlasting than my own. I've been there. Inescapably, I am the American soldier in Beirut. . . .

NIGHT IS ALWAYS THE HARDEST TIME *when you are far from home. The mind has time to wander and remember, playing its fiendish tricks. Time passes more slowly and the darkness beckons you into the depths of its unyielding control. Memories are friend and foe.*

He had been away too long and he knew it, but the job was not done and the stillness of the night only reminded him of that. It was funny how quiet the nights could be. Leaning back and allowing the mind to take over brought him to quiet times at home with family. . .and yeah, back to her. He'd be back home, he knew, and silence would return again.

He chuckled to himself at being called a "peacekeeper" when there had been no peace since his arrival. The night reverberated with the echoes of the day's fighting, and he wondered if the sound would ever go away.

The soldier gave a quick wink to the heavens in their celestial migration toward his home, shifted his gun and continued his guard. The job was not done.

ON OCTOBER 23, 1983, the stillness of the Beirut night erupted into the hellfire of a suicide-bomber attack against the headquarters of the United States peacekeeping forces. In its wake, 240 men were dead.

Before the monuments are built, this unembellished roll call of our lost guardian warriors will serve as testimony to their legacy of honor, pride and dignity.

Killed in Action

Cpl. Terry Abbott	New Richmond, OH	USMC
L. Cpl. Clemon Alexander	Monticello, FL	USMC
Pfc John Allman	Carlsbad, NM	USMC
Cpl. M. Arnold	Philadelphia, PA	USMC
Pfc Charles Bailey	Berlin, MD	USMC
L. Cpl. Nicholas Baker	Alexandria, VA	USMC
L. Cpl. Johansen Banks	Detroit, MI	USMC
L. Cpl. Richard Barrett	Tappahanock, VA	USMC
HM 1 Ronny K. Bates	Aiken, SC	USN
1st Sgt. D.L. Battle	Hubert, NC	USMC
L. Cpl. James Baynard	Richmond, VA	USMC
HN Jesse W. Beamon	Haines City, FL	USN
Gy. Sgt. Alvin Belmer	Jacksonville, NC	USMC
Pfc Stephen Bland	Midway Park, NC	USMC
Cpl. Richard Blankenship	Hubert, NC	USMC
Pfc John Blocker	Yulee, FL	USMC
Capt. Joseph Boccia, Jr.	Northport, NY	USMC
Cpl. Leon Bohannon	Jacksonville, NC	USMC
S. Sgt. John Bohnet	Memphis, TN	USMC
Cpl. John Bonk, Jr.	Philadelphia, PA	USMC
L. Cpl. Jeffrey Boulos	Islip, NY	USMC
Cpl. David Bousum	Fife Lake, MI	USMC
1st Lt. John Boyett	Camp Lejeune, NC	USMC
Cpl. Anthony Brown	Detroit, MI	USMC
L. Cpl. David Brown	Conroe, TX	USMC
L. Cpl. Bobby Buchanan, Jr.	Midway Park, NC	USMC
Cpl. John Buckmaster	Vandalia, OH	USMC
Pfc William Burley	Linden, NJ	USMC
HN Jimmy R. Cain	Birmingham, AL	USN
Cpl. Paul Callahan	Lorain, OH	USMC
Cpl. M.E. Camara	Jacksonville, NC	USMC

Pfc Bradley Campus	Lynn, MA	USMC
L. Cpl. Johnnie Ceasar	El Campo, TX	USMC
Pfc Marc Cole	Ludlow Falls, OH	USMC
SP4 Marcus E. Coleman	Dallas, TX	US Army
Pfc Juan Comas	Hialeah, FL	USMC
Sgt. Robert Conley	Orlando, FL	USMC
Cpl. Charles Cook	Advance, NC	USMC
L. Cpl. Johnny Copeland	Burlington, NC	USMC
Cpl. Bert Corcoran	Katonah, NY	USMC
L. Cpl. David Cosner	Elkins, WVA	USMC
Sgt. Kevin Coulman	Seminary, NY	USMC
L. Cpl. Brett Croft	Lakeland, FL	USMC
L. Cpl. Rick Crudale	W. Warwick, RI	USMC
L. Cpl. Kevin Custard	Virg ia, MN	USMC
L. Cpl. Russell Cyzick	Star City, WVA	USMC
Maj. Andrew Davis	Jacksonville, NC	USMC
Pfc Sidney Decker	Clarkston, KY	USMC
Pfc Michael Devlin	Westwood, MA	USMC
L. Cpl. T. Dibenedetto	Mansfield Center, CT	USMC
Pvt. Nathaniel Dorsey	Baltimore, MD	USMC
Sgt. Maj. F.B. Douglass	Cataumet, MA	USMC
Cpl. Timothy Dunnigan	Princeton, WV	USMC
HN Bryan L. Earle	Painesville, OH	USN
M. Sgt. Roy Edwards	Camp Lejeune, NC	USMC
HM3 William D. Elliot, Jr.	Lancaster, PA	USN
L. Cpl. Jesse Ellison	Soldiers Grove, WI	USMC
Pfc Danny Estes	Gary, IN	USMC
Pfc Sean Estler	Kendall Park, NJ	USMC
HM3 James E. Faulk	Panama City, FL	USN
Pfc Richard Fluegel	Erie, PA	USMC
Cpl. Steven Forrester	Jacksonville, NC	USMC
HM3 William Foster, Jr.	Richmond, GA	USN
Cpl. Michael Fulcher	Madison Heights, VA	USMC
L. Cpl. Benjamin Fuller	Duluth, GA	USMC
L. Cpl. Michael Fulton	Forth Worth, TX	USMC
Cpl. William Gaines, Jr.	Fort Charlotte, FL	USMC
L. Cpl. Sean Gallagher	N. Andover, MA	USMC
L. Cpl. David Gander	Milwaukee, WI	USMC
L. Cpl. George Gangur	Cleveland, OH	USMC
S. Sgt. Leland Gann	Camp Lejeune, NC	USMC
L. Cpl. Randall Garcia	Modesto, CA	USMC

S. Sgt. Ronald Garcia	Jacksonville, NC	USMC
L. Cpl. David Gay	Jacksonville, NC	USMC
S. Sgt. Harold Ghumm	Jacksonville, NC	USMC
L. Cpl. Warner Gibbs	Portsmouth, VA	USMC
Cpl. Timothy Giblin	N. Providence, RI	USMC
L. Cpl. Richard Gordon	Somerville, MA	USMC
ETC Michael W. Gorchinski	Evansville, IN	USN
L. Cpl. Harold Gratton	Conoes, NY	USMC
Sgt. Robert Greaser	Lansdale, PA	USMC
L. Cpl. D.M. Green	Baltimore, MD	USMC
L. Cpl. Thomas Hairston	Philadelphia, PA	USMC
Sgt. Freddie Haltiwanger, Jr.	Little Mountain, SC	USMC
L. Cpl. Virgil Hamilton	McDowell, KY	USMC
Sgt. Gilbert Hanton	Washington, D.C.	USMC
L. Cpl. William Hart	Jacksonville, NC	USMC
Capt. Michael Haskell	Camp Lejeune, NC	USMC
Pfc Michael Hastings	Seaford, DE	USMC
Capt. Paul Hein	Camp Lejeune, NC	USMC
L. Cpl. Douglas Held	Jacksonville, NC	USMC
Pfc Mark Helms	Dwight, NE	USMC
L. Cpl. Ferrandy Henderson	Tampa, FL	USMC
Gy. Sgt. Matilde Hernandez, Jr.	Midway Park, NC	USMC
Cpl. Stanley Hester	Raleigh, NC	USMC
Gy. Sgt. D.W. Hildreth	Sneads Ferry, NC	USMC
S. Sgt. Richard Holberton	Beaufort, SC	USMC
HM3 Robert S. Holland	Gilbertsville, KY	USN
L. Cpl. Bruce Hollingshead	Fairborn, OH	USMC
Pfc Melvin Holmes	Chicago, IL	USMC
Cpl. Bruce Howard	Strong, ME	USMC
Lt. John R. Hudson	Riverdale, GA	USN
L. Cpl. Terry L. Hudson	Prichard, AL	USMC
L. Cpl. Lyndon Hue	Des Allemands, LA	USMC
2d Lt. Maurice Hukill	Jacksonville, NC	USMC
L. Cpl. Edward Iacovino, Jr.	Warwick, RI	USMC
Pfc John Ingalls	Interlaken, NY	USMC
WO-1 Paul Innocenzi	Trenton, NJ	USMC
L. Cpl. James Jackowski	S. Salem, NY	USMC
L. Cpl. Jeffrey James	Baltimore, MD	USMC
L. Cpl. Nathaniel Jenkins	Daytona Beach, FL	USMC
HM2 Michael H. Johnson	Detroit, MI	USN
Cpl. Edward Johnston	Struthers, OH	USMC

L. Cpl. Steven Jones	Brooklyn, NY	USMC
Pfc Thomas Julian	Middleton, RI	USMC
HM2 Marlon E. Kees	Martinsburg, WV	USN
Sgt. Thomas Keown	Louisville, KY	USMC
Gy. Sgt. E. Kimm	Atlantic, IA	USMC
L. Cpl. Walter Kingsley	Wisconsin Dells, WI	USMC
Sgt. Daniel S. Kluck	Owensboro, KY	US Army
L. Cpl. James Knipple	Alexandria, VA	USMC
L. Cpl. F.H. Kreischer, III	Indialantic, FL	USMC
L. Cpl. Keith Laise	Stroudsburgh, PA	USMC
L. Cpl. Thomas Lamb	Coon Rapids, MN	USMC
Cpl. J.J. Langon	Lakehurst, NJ	USMC
Sgt. Michael Lariviere	Perry, FL	USMC
Cpl. Steven Lariviere	Chicopee, MA	USMC
M. Sgt. Richard Lemnah	Camp Lejeune, NC	USMC
Cpl. David Lewis	Garfield Heights, OH	USMC
Sgt. Val Lewis	Atlanta, GA	USMC
L. Cpl. Paul Lyon, Jr.	Milton, FL	USMC
Maj. John Macroglou	Jacksonville, NC	USMC
Cpl. Samuel Maitland	Jacksonville, NC	USMC
S. Sgt. Charlie Martin	Camp Lejeune, NC	USMC
Pfc Jack Martin	Oveido, FL	USMC
Cpl. David Massa	Warren, RI	USMC
Cpl. Michael Massman	Jacksonville, NC	USMC
Pvt. Joseph Mattacchione	Sanford, NC	USMC
L. Cpl. John McCall	Rochester, NY	USMC
Cpl. James McDonough	Newcastle, PA	USMC
Pfc Timothy McMahon	Austin, TX	USMC
L. Cpl. Timothy McNeely	Mooresville, NC	USMC
HM2 George N. McVicker II	Wabash, IN	USN
Pfc Louis Melendez	Santa Marie Calle, PR	USMC
Sgt. Michael Mercer	Vale, NC	USMC
L. Cpl. Ronald Meurer	Jacksonville, NC	USMC
HM3 Joseph P. Milano	Farmingvale, NY	USN
Cpl. Joseph Moore	St. Louis, MO	USMC
L. Cpl. Richard Morrow	Clairton, PA	USMC
L. Cpl. John Muffler	Philadelphia, PA	USMC
Pfc Alex Munoz	Bloomfield, NM	USMC
Cpl. Harry Myers	Whittler, NC	USMC
1st Lt. David Nairn	Jacksonville, NC	USMC
L. Cpl. Luis Nava	Gardena, CA	USMC

Cpl. John Olson	Sabin, MN	USMC
Pfc Robert Olson	Lawtons, NY	USMC
CWO-3 Richard Ortiz	Ft. Sill, OK	USMC
L. Cpl. J.B. Owen	Virginia Beach, VA	USMC
Cpl. Joseph Owens	Chesterfield, VA	USMC
Cpl. Ray Page	Erwin, NC	USMC
L. Cpl. Ulysses Parker	Baltimore, MD	USMC
L. Cpl. Mark Payne	Binghamton, NY	USMC
Gy. Sgt. John Pearson	Jacksonville, NC	USMC
Pfc Thomas Perron	Whitinsville, MA	USMC
Sgt. John Phillips, Jr.	Wilmette, IL	USMC
HMC George W. Piercy	Mt. Savage, MD	USN
1st Lt. Clyde Plymel	Merritt, FL	USMC
Sgt. William Pollard	Jacksonville, NC	USMC
Sgt. Rafael Pomalestorres	Philadelphia, PA	USMC
Cpl. Victor Prevatt	Columbus, GA	USMC
Pfc James Price	Attala, AL	USMC
S. Sgt. Patrick Prindeville	Gainesville, FL	USMC
Pfc Eric Pulliam	E. St. Louis, MO	USMC
HM3 Diomeded J. Quirante	Calcoocan City, R. Phillipines	USN
Gy. Sgt. Charles Ray	Camp Lejeune, NC	USMC
Pfc R.A. Relvas	Philadelphia, PA	USMC
Pfc Terrence Rich	Brooklyn, NY	USMC
L. Cpl. Warren Richardson	Brooklyn, NY	USMC
Cpl. Paul Rivers	Brooklyn, NY	USMC
Sgt. Juan Rodriguez	Miami, FL	USMC
L. Cpl. Louis Rotondo	Philadelphia, PA	USMC
L. Cpl. B. Sandpedro	Haileah, FL	USMC
HM3 James Saulk	Panama City, FL	USN
L. Cpl. Michael Sauls	Waterboro, SC	USMC
1st Lt. Charles Schnorf	Camp Lejeune, NC	USMC
Pfc Scott Schultz	Keeseville, NY	USMC
Capt. Peter Scialabba	Moorehead City, NC	USMC
Cpl. Gary Scott	Rankin, IL	USMC
Cpl. Ronald Shallo	Hudson, NY	USMC
L. Cpl. Thomas Shipp	Jacksonville, NC	USMC
Pfc Jerryl Shropshire	Macon, GA	USMC
L. Cpl. James Silvia	Portsmouth, RI	USMC
L. Cpl. Stanley Sliwinski	Niles, OH	USMC
L. Cpl. Kirk Smith	Miami, FL	USMC

S. Sgt. Thomas Smith	Middletown, CT	USMC
Capt. Vincent Smith	Jacksonville, NC	USMC
L. Cpl. Edward Soares	Riverton, RI	USMC
1st Lt. William Sommerhof	Springfield, IL	USMC
L. Cpl. Michael Spaulding	Akron, OH	USMC
L. Cpl. John Spearing	Lancaster, PA	USMC
L. Cpl. Stephen Spencer	Portsmouth, RI	USMC
Pfc Bill Stelpflug	Auburn, AL	USMC
Pfc Horace Stephens	Capital Heights, MD	USMC
Pfc Craig Stockton	Rochester, NY	USMC
L. Cpl. Jeffrey Stokes	Waynesboro, GA	USMC
L. Cpl. Thomas Stowe	Jacksonville, NC	USMC
L. Cpl. Eric Sturghill	Chicago, IL	USMC
Lt. James F. Surch, Jr.	Lampoc, CA	USN
L. Cpl. Devon Sundar	Stanford, CT	USMC
Cpl. Dennis Thompson	Bronx, NY	USMC
S. Sgt. Thomas Thorstad	Chesterson, IN	USMC
Pfc Stephen Tingley	Ellington, CT	USMC
L. Cpl. John Tishmack	Minneapolis, MN	USMC
Pvt. L.D. Trahan	Lafayette, LA	USMC
Pfc Donald Vallone, Jr.	Palmdale, CA	USMC
L. Cpl. Eric Walker	Chicago, IL	USMC
L. Cpl. Leonard Walker	Dothan, AL	USMC
Cpl. Eric Washington	Alexandria, VA	USMC
Cpl. Obrian Weekes	Brooklyn, NY	USMC
1st Sgt. Tandy Wells	Jacksonville, NC	USMC
L. Cpl. Steven Wentworth	Reading, PA	USMC
Sgt. Allen Wesley	Philadelphia, PA	USMC
Gy. Sgt. Lloyd West	Jacksonville, NC	USMC
S. Sgt. John Weyl	Jacksonville, NC	USMC
Cpl. Burton Wherland	Jacksonville, NC	USMC
L. Cpl. Dwayne Wigglesworth	Naugutuck, CT	USMC
L. Cpl. Rodney Williams	Opa Locka, FL	USMC
Gy. Sgt. Scipio Williams	Charleston, SC	USMC
L. Cpl. Johnny A. Williamson	Asheboro, NC	USMC
Capt. Walter Wint, Jr.	Wilkes-Barre, PA	USMC
Capt. William Winter	Fripp Island, SC	USMC
Cpl. John Wolfe	Phoenix, AZ	USMC
1st Lt. Donald Woollett	Barthesville, OK	USMC
HM3 David E. Worley	Baltimore, MD	USN
Pfc Craig Wyche	Jamaica, NY	USMC

Sfc James G. Yarber	Vacaville, CA	USArmy
Cpl. Jeffrey Young	Morrestown, NJ	USMC
1st Lt. William Zimmerman	Grand Haven, MI	USMC

Missing

L. Cpl. Curtis Cooper	North Wales, PA	USMC
L. Cpl. David Randolph	Siloam Springs, AR	USMC

Wounded

L. Cpl. Marvin Albright	Bridgeport, CT	USMC
HN Lorenzo Almanza	El Paso, TX	USN
HN Pedro Alvarado	Ponce, PR	USN
L. Cpl. Dennis Anderson	Kennesaw, GA	USMC
Sgt. Pablo Arroyo	Bronx, NY	USMC
Pfc Michael Balcom	Vernon, NY	USMC
L. Cpl. Anthony Banks	St. Louis, MO	USMC
HM3 Donald Basley	Cochran, GA	USN
Cpl. Neale Bolen	Cedarlake, IN	USMC
L. Cpl. Thomas Brown	Palatka, FL	USMC
Cpl. Rodney Burnette	Charlotte, NC	USMC
Pfc Rodney Burns	St. Peters, MO	USMC
1st Lt. Charles Dallachie	Milford, CT	USMC
Pfc Anthony Darrington	Selma, AL	USMC
L. Cpl. Steven Diaz	Chicago, IL	USMC
Cpl. James Donohue	Bethpage, NY	USMC
L. Cpl. Morris Dorsey	Poughkeepsie, NY	USMC
L. Cpl. James Dudney	Millersville, MD	USMC
HM3 Ronald L. Duplanty	Flint, MI	USN
Cpl. Brook Ehrenfried	Newport News, VA	USMC
Gy. Sgt. Evan Fain	New River, NC	USMC
L. Cpl. John Foster	Robbins, IL	USMC
Cpl. Truman Garner	Parrish, AL	USMC
Lt. Col. Howard Gerlach	Jacksonville, NC	USMC
Sgt. John Gibson	Jacksonville, NC	USMC
L. Cpl. Earl Guy	Dayton, OH	USMC
L. Cpl. Michael Harris	Woonsocket, MI	USMC
L. Cpl. Wayne Harris	Richmond, VA	USMC
Sfc Elvin H. Henry, Jr.	Columbia, SC	US Army
Cpl. James Hines	Forrest City, IA	USMC
HM3 Donald A. Howell	Charleston Heights, SC	USN
S. Sgt. Orval Hunt	Camp Lejeune, NC	USMC

Sgt. Jesse James	Hubert, NC	USMC
HM1 Larry W. Jenkins	Pontiac, MI	USN
L. Cpl. Kevin Jiggetts	Suitland, MD	USMC
Gy. Sgt. Ronald Jones	Jacksonville, NC	USMC
L. Cpl. John Kinslow	Valley City, ND	USMC
Cpl. Brian Kirkpatrick	Camp Lejeune, NC	USMC
Gy. Sgt. Herman Lange	San Diego, CA	USMC
Sgt. Tommy Laster	Albany, GA	USMC
L. Cpl. John Lheureux	Randolph, MA	USMC
Sgt. Donald Long	Jacksonville, NC	USMC
L. Cpl. Renard Manley	Delray Beach, FL	USMC
L. Cpl. Burnham Matthews	Odenton, MD	USMC
L. Cpl. Charles Melefsky	Frackville, PA	USMC
L. Cpl. Timothy Mitchell	Baltimore, MD	USMC
L. Cpl. Lovelle Moore	E. St. Louis, IL	USMC
1st Lt. Aineal Morris	Sarasota, FL	USMC
L. Cpl. Jeffrey Nashton	Jacksonville, NC	USMC
Pfc Joe Nichols	Detroit, MI	USMC
Gy. Sgt. Winston Oxendine	Johnson City, TN	USMC
L. Cpl. Michael Page	Mansfield, OH	USMC
Cpl. Samuel Palmer	Covington, VA	USMC
L. Cpl. Michael Parris	Sneads Ferry, NC	USMC
L. Cpl. David Rollison	Waymart, PA	USMC
Sgt. Steve Russell	Camp Lejeune, NC	USMC
Cpl. John Santos	Sandwich, MA	USMC
Cpl. Joseph Schneider	Pensacola, FL	USMC
Sgt. John Selbe	Marmet, WV	USMC
Cpl. Thurnell Shields	Savannah, GA	USMC
L. Cpl. Emanuel Simmons	New York, NY	USMC
L. Cpl. Larry Simpson	Amity, PA	USMC
Cpl. Dana Spaudling	Batavia, NY	USMC
L. Cpl. Albert Thompkins	Jacksonville, NC	USMC
L. Cpl. Willie Thompson	Cross, SC	USMC
L. Cpl. Michael Toma	Elwood City, PA	USMC
Cpl. Henry Townsend	Montgomery, AL	USMC
Cpl. Terance Valore	Slickville, PA	USMC
HN John J. Vaughn	Gadsden, AL	USN
L. Cpl. Jamie Velasco	Milwaukee, WI	USMC
Cpl. Joseph Vincent	Virginia Beach, VA	USMC
L. Cpl. Adam Webb	Jacobsburg, OH	USMC
Cpl. Galen Weber	Waite Park, MN	USMC

LTJG Dan G. Wheeler	Menomonie, WI	USN
S. Sgt. Norman Whetham	Jacksonville, NC	USMC
Cpl. David Wilcox	Machias, ME	USMC
Sgt. Armando Ybarra	Jacksonville, NC	USMC

Born of the cause,
And raised from the need.
United in the fire,
And separated by none.
The lone warrior guards the graves
and begins the day of mourning.

ABLE TEAM
AND
PHOENIX FORCE

Able Team:
Superexcellence in action

Remember Able Team #3: *Texas Showdown*? See if these hot new words from Dick Stivers bring back a flash from that memorable book....

ROCKET STRIKES LIT THE DISTANT ESTATE, lines of flame shooting from the unseen helicopter, simultaneous flashes lighting the mountaintop. The sound of the explosions came seconds later.

Lyons watched the attack. He crouched near the open hangar door, shielded from the attackers' autofire by the steel of the forklift. After the first rocket blasts, the firefight had died away.

His hand-radio buzzed. "Grimaldi here," the Stony Man pilot shouted over the helicopter noise. "They're all gone. On my way to give assistance to you leg soldiers."

Scanning the starlit darkness of the airfield for gunmen, Carl Lyons flicked his hand-radio's frequency over to the mercenary frequency. "Soldiers! Surrender! Look up at the Monroe house. It's gone. Monroe is dead, the Mexicans are dead. It's all over."

No response came. No voices answered him on the radio. He waited for rifle fire. But he heard none. He slipped from behind the forklift and crossed the distance to the steel panels of the hangar door. He crouched there, then shouted into the darkness. "It's all over. They're all dead. There's no reason to fight. Federal officers will be here in minutes."

"Why shouldn't we kill you?" a voice called out. "We're already up against murder one. Multiple murder."

Lyons recognized the voice of the six-foot-eight Sergeant Cooke. "Who'd you kill, Cooke? Did you kill Federal officers? Did you do the torture?"

"No, but I killed some Mexican dopers," the sergeant yelled back.

"Outside United States jurisdiction," Lyons shouted. "Cooperate with the investigation and you'll be free in a few days. Maybe they'll give you a citizen's commendation for fighting the international heroin business!"

"Hey, Fed!" another man shouted. "I'm on the run for armed robbery of a bank. If I stop shooting at you, can we make a deal?"

"That's between you and the bank. If you want to risk the desert, keep running."

Another soldier shouted, "We can't give up. Furst and Pardee and their psychos will shoot us down. They got nothing to lose."

"Furst and Pardee are dead!" Lyons shouted back. "All the leaders are dead—"

An arm locked around Lyons's neck. As the arm lifted Lyons from his feet, Pardee's voice rasped in his ear, "Wrong, Federal. I'm alive, and you're going to die with your balls down your throat."

The ironlike arm tightened around his throat, taking away Lyons's breath. His pulse pounded in his head. He tried to call out, could not. Striking wildly, he hammered Pardee's concrete-hard body, clawed at his uniform. Pardee dragged him outside.

Lyons felt his consciousness slipping away. Lights swirled in his vision as he started to die. He flailed his arms in a desperate frenzy.

Pardee stood at the side of the hangar, his arm clamped around Lyons's neck.

"This is Commander Pardee!" he bellowed to his soldiers. "There's only two Federals left in there. Rush them! Kill them!"

Blancanales leaned from the hangar entry, leveling his rifle for a careful shot at Pardee's head.

Jerking his Colt automatic from his web belt, Pardee swung Lyons around to shield himself. Blancanales dived back as .45-caliber slugs smashed the steel.

"Kill the Federals!" Pardee commanded again.

No one moved. Not a rifle fired.

"Thompson! McBain! Get your men moving!"

One of the squad leaders shouted at his men. He fired his M-16 into the air. "Up and moving! Put down those Feds!"

"You do it!" a soldier told him from the shadows.

McBain fired his rifle at the soldier. A burst of autofire answered him. McBain scrambled for cover.

Others soldiers fired. A slug zipped past Pardee. He dodged sideways. Lyons reached over his shoulder. He felt his fingers go into Pardee's eye and Lyons clawed.

Pardee screamed and twisted his face away, his arm around Lyons's throat going slack for an instant. Lyons broke free. Blind with oxygen starvation, every gasp an agony, he stumbled across the asphalt. His head slammed into a parked truck.

Slugs punched steel, broke glass. Lyons rolled under the truck, sucking down breath after breath. His vision returned. He heard a soldier shouting, "Waste that motherfuck Pardee! Blow his ass away—"

A shot killed the soldier. Pardee shouted again. "Listen to me! We got the helicopters, we got our weapons. We can kill these worms, bc gone before their backup makes it here.

There's only three of them—they don't have any backup closer than El Paso. We can break out—"

Rotorthrob overwhelmed his words. The converted helicopter swept in low, then soared up to a few hundred feet and hovered. A rifle fired a burst.

Lyons crawled from under the parked truck. He could breathe now. He pulled his six-inch magna-ported Colt Python from his shoulder holster. He looked back toward the hangar for Pardee.

One soldier sprawled on the asphalt. All the others—including Pardee—had taken cover. Approximately fifty feet separated Lyons from the second hangar where Blancanales and Gadgets waited for the battle to resume. Hundreds of yards beyond, near the gate, a truck burned.

The helicopter angled away. Red firelight from the burning trucks flashed on the helicopter's rotors as it circled the third hangar, the last in the row of three hangars. Grimaldi aimed the side door at the third hangar.

Rockets blew the steel prefab to scrap. A vast blossom of flaming aviation fuel rose into the night sky. Lyons felt the flame on his face. The helicopter roared past him.

The first hangar disintegrated in a chain of rocket blasts. Then the helicopter wheeled away to circle the landing field.

Blancanales called out from the door of the last hangar, "Surrender or die. When the gunship comes back, he kills you all! Throw down your weapons or die!"

Pardee shouted, "I'll kill any man who gives up!"

Lyons fixed the voice. He dropped to a crouch and watched the shadows along the side of the hangar. Rifle fire, not aimed at Able Team's Gadgets or Blancanales but at Pardee, punched the sheet steel. Lyons saw a pistol flash and heard the report of a Colt automatic. He leveled his Python at the shadow and fired.

A pistol answered his shot, .45 slugs smashing into the van

that shielded Lyons. Lyons fired twice at the flashing pistol. Pardee broke from the shadows and ran for the back of the hangar. Lyons braced his pistol in both hands and sighted on Pardee's running form.

The shot spun Pardee. He fell, then scrambled up and ran again. Lyons broke cover, grabbing a speedloader from his fatigue pants' side pocket. He sprinted after Pardee.

Rifle slugs zipped past Lyons. He saw a shadow with a rifle and snapped two shots. The rifle did not fire again.

Running to the corner of the hangar building, Lyons stopped short. He squatted and snapped a glance around the corner. He saw a movement in the shadows and aimed his Python.

An autopistol flashed twice, one slug slamming into the corrugated steel of the hangar, the other roaring past Lyons's ear. Lyons held his position and fired at the flashing Colt in Pardee's hands.

Pardee staggered backward but did not fall. Lyons flipped open the Python's cylinder, popped out the brass and slapped in the speedloader's six cartridges. But before he could fire again, Pardee lurched around the corner of the hangar.

Lyons knew he had hit Pardee twice, the second shot a torso hit. The 158-grain hollowpoint slugs, traveling at 1300 feet per second, should have killed Pardee. . . .

Unless he wore high-quality Kevlar body armor.

Following the wounded man, Lyons heard Pardee call out to his soldiers, "There's only three of them! Three Federals standing between you and freedom. Are you going to let three cops take all of you to prison? We can get out of here! We can go anywhere in the world!"

A soldier shouted from the flame-lit darkness. "Remember kicking my ass, Pardee? Remember stomping on me?"

A long burst of 5.56mm slugs ripped through Pardee's legs, the impacts spraying bone and flesh, throwing the huge man to the asphalt. Blood pooled around his shattered, twisted legs. He lay still, making no sound.

"Won't do it anymore, will you?" the soldier taunted. Laughing, he left the darkness and advanced on Pardee. He dropped the magazine from his M-16 and fumbled to insert another.

Pardee shot the man in the face, the slug blowing away the back of the soldier's head, throwing the man onto his back to flop and thrash as his nerves died.

Other rifles fired, Pardee's arm flailing suddenly, the Colt automatic clattering away. Clawing at the asphalt, Pardee tried to drag himself to his pistol. A rifle fired again.

Pardee screamed in agony and hatred, his cry fading away in a gurgle of blood. Lyons sprinted to the dying man and kicked the pistol away.

Blood bubbled from Pardee's mouth. The 5.56mm military slugs, full-jacketed and traveling at a velocity of 3200 feet per second, had punched through his Kevlar vest to score his lungs. His other wounds—his legs shredded by autobursts, his right forearm hanging from the shattered elbow by tendons and strands of muscle—poured blood into a spreading pool.

Pardee opened his eyes as Lyons leaned over him. His left hand grabbed Lyons's throat and pulled his face down.

"I won't be a prisoner," Pardee gasped, blood from his words spraying Lyons's face. "You're not going to take me to a hospital . . . no prison for me. . . . Kill me."

"Suffer, bad man. Like you made those two Federal officers suffer."

"I fought for our country. My country called me and I went like a man. I didn't read the fine print and I didn't cry to my Congressman. I deserve to die like a soldier. . . ."

Pardee choked on his blood. He turned his head to the side and spat out gore. He sucked down another breath and continued his proud words. "I don't want to go to hell knowing those losers and cowards sent me. You kill me. I deserve to be put away by a soldier, even if he's a Federal. I'd do the same for you."

Lyons looked into the face of the dying man. "You got it, Pardee. Close your eyes and pray to whoever you call God—"

"Screw that. I'll look death in face. And when you die, I'll be waiting for you on the right hand of Satan!"

Standing, Lyons aimed at the center of Craig Pardee's forehead. The mercy of a high-velocity hollowpoint put him beyond this world of pain and betrayal.

Fly with Phoenix Force!

An excerpt from Phoenix Force #10: *Korean Killground*.

THE CHOPPER SWUNG ABOUT low in the valley, its light splashing the small farmhouse a few seconds longer than normal. Katz saw something, stiffened, then exhaled an enraged gasp. *"Du kucker!"* he groaned, a strong oath indeed for Katz. *"Du kuckteppel!"*

"Yakov," Encizo said solicitiously, "*¿qué cosa?* What is it?"

"The swine," their leader grated, his voice breaking with emotion. "Look! The filthy inhuman swine!"

Three men were drawing up a lifeless, horribly mutilated body to the helicopter with a rope. Suspended from a crossbeam, in full view of the public road, it was the corpse of Young Sam. This was the brave Korean's final humiliation.

In that fleeting, floodlit moment it was all branded in the memory; nothing would ever erase those grotesque images. Chang's head was awash with blood where the cheated officer—transformed to raving psycho—had kicked it in. Arrow shafts protruded from the eye sockets. His genitals were missing, where the savages had hacked at his crotch. And the arrow—dear God, look where it was!

What kind of degenerates were these? Yakov lowered his eyes, began to retch. He shuddered uncontrollably. Control, he adjured, I must get control of myself.

"Filthy bloody slime," McCarter hissed as he grabbed the binoculars. He fought with all his strength to suppress the rage that threatened to consume him. "I'll make them pay for this, I swear. I'll tear out their hearts with my bare hands. They'll pay!"

And when it was Encizo's turn: "That poor, game little bastard," he said, his voice muffled. His head slumped forward, his hands clenched and unclenched. Under his breath he said some rapid prayers in Spanish.

Ohara said nothing. He mutely passed the glasses to Manning, then turned away. His glazed eyes had caught the horror in lasting detail; now his jaws worked, and his face was rock hard.

"Well?" McCarter glowered when they had all regained adequate composure. "Now do we go after the scum?"

Katz regarded his Brit comrade with patient sympathy. He wished it could be. If only there was a way. But there was not. They were wildly outnumbered. The armed helicopter would cut them to shreds the moment they exposed themselves.

"Our plan is still the same," he said softly. "We survive. We honor Young Sam for his terrible sacrifice."

"Goddamn it, guv," McCarter railed, "we must avenge Young Sam."

"And if we all die?"

"Die? I'd rather be dead than live with the thought that I deserted a friend. That...thing...will be inside my head forever. And when I remember I did nothing about it...."

Katz laid his arm across the hotheaded brawler's shoulder. "I know how you feel, David," he said. "I feel the same way. But it cannot be. It will solve nothing."

"So?" Gary Manning said, his eyes resentful. "What *do* we do?"

"We wait for an opening. And when the time is right..." Yakov sighed softly. "We move. With any kind of luck we just might take a few of them with us." He hefted the silenced Makarov pistol meaningfully.

Katz realized with profound feeling that his men had become the ultimate soldiers. They did not follow orders blindly; instead, each man was calmly tactical and analytical in the heart of danger. Yet at this time, against all odds, they persisted in taking a course of action that could only spell the annihilation of Phoenix Force. Katz knew that they had developed an undying affection for the pint-sized Korean. Even Keio Ohara, with his deep-seated resentment of Koreans, had begun to relent in his attitude toward Chang Young Sam.

The ex-Mossad agent came to a chilling realization. Manning, McCarter, Encizo and Ohara did not want just blind revenge. Their seething rage ran far deeper than the avenging of their Korean friend.

The psychopathic butchering of Chang had precipitated the eruption of his men's simmering rage about the slaying of April Rose, their Virginia headquarters' primary mission controller and overseer. . . .

Let it happen, he thought to himself. So let them unleash the fury!

WEAPONS IN REVIEW

Beginning with Mack Bolan #64: *Dead Man Running* and Able Team #11: *Five Rings of Fire*, Gold Eagle will be presenting Weapons in Review on the inside back covers of all forthcoming Mack Bolan, Able Team and Phoenix Force books.

Weapons in Review is a numbered series of illustrations displaying weapons and weapon systems from all over the world, some so advanced they have not been shown in a public forum before.

The weapons will be appearing in the stories themselves, but the inside back cover of every book in the Mack Bolan and spin-off series will be the only place you can *see* the armament in vivid detail, with thrilling up-to-the-minute data on each.

Start your collection now! Suitable for album mounting or framing.

DON PENDLETON'S EXECUTIONER
MACK BOLAN

Sergeant Mercy in Nam...The Executioner in the Mafia Wars...Colonel John Phoenix in the Terrorist Wars.... Now Mack Bolan fights his loneliest war! You've never read writing like this before. Faceless dogsoldiers have killed April Rose. The Executioner's one link with compassion is broken. His path is clear: by fire and maneuver, he will rack up hell in a world shock-tilted by terror. Bolan wages unsanctioned war—everywhere!

GOLD EAGLE

Available wherever paperbacks are sold.

Mack Bolan's

ABLE TEAM

by Dick Stivers

Action writhes in the reader's own street as Able Team's Carl "Mr. Ironman" Lyons, Pol Blancanales and Gadgets Schwarz make triple trouble in blazing war. To these superspecialists, justice is as sharp as a knife. Join the guys who began it all—Dick Stivers's Able Team!

"This guy has a fertile mind and a great eye for detail. Dick Stivers is brilliant!"

—*Don Pendleton*

Able Team titles are available wherever paperbacks are sold.

GOLD EAGLE

Mack Bolan's

PHOENIX FORCE

by Gar Wilson

Schooled in guerilla warfare, equipped with all the latest
lethal hardware, Phoenix Force battles the powers of
darkness in an endless crusade for freedom, justice and
the rights of the individual. Follow the adventures of one
of the legends of the genre. Phoenix Force is the free
world's foreign legion!

"Gar Wilson is excellent! Raw action attacks the reader
on every page."

—Don Pendleton

#1 Argentine Deadline	#6 White Hell
#2 Guerilla Games	#7 Dragon's Kill
#3 Atlantic Scramble	#8 Aswan Hellbox
#4 Tigers of Justice	#9 Ultimate Terror
#5 The Fury Bombs	#10 Korean Killground

GOLD
EAGLE

Phoenix Force titles are available
wherever paperbacks are sold.

BOLAN FIGHTS
AGAINST ALL ODDS
TO DEFEND FREEDOM

Mail this coupon today!